A Little Way of Homeschooling

A Little Way of Homeschooling

Thirteen Families Discover Catholic Unschooling

by Suzie Andres

Foreword by Mike Aquilina

Contributions by:
Cindy Kelly
Amy Wagner
Leonie Westenberg
Terri Aquilina
Maria Peceli
Beate and Sabine
Susan Fuerst
Karen Edmisten
Faith Roberts
Melissa Wiley
Willa Ryan

Appendix by Tony Andres

Cover design by Ted Schluenderfritz
Book design by Nora Malone

Library of Congress Catologing-in-Publication data available on request.

Hillside Education
475 Bidwell Hill Road
Lake Ariel, PA 18436
www.hillsideeducation.com

Jesus does not demand great actions from us
but simply *surrender* and *gratitude*.

—St. Thérèse of Lisieux, *Story of a Soul*

With deepest gratitude
to my dear ladies:
Cindy, Amy, Leonie, Terri,
Maria, Beate and Sabine, Susan,
Karen, Faith, Lissa,
and Willa

&

With all my love
to Emily,
whose friendship is like
sunshine

Contents

Part One: Catholic Unschooling

Part Two: Catholic Unschoolers

Part Three: More Catholic Unschoolers

Appendices

Foreword

Mike Aquilina

Suzie Andres is right: unschooling is not an ideology. But at one time I was prepared to dismiss it as one. When my wife started reading John Holt, the notion seemed a little hippy-dippy to me—a little too Rousseau. Where's the allowance for original sin? How would the kids get over their laziness and concupiscence if we just let them follow their bliss all the livelong day? Rousseau had gone a long way with his talk about "noble savages" because he was addressing civilized folks to whom "savages" were a theoretical proposition. And John Holt, I pointed out, had never had children of his own.

I lived with my savages, and I would not be easily fooled.

By this time in our marriage, however, I had learned an important lesson. I'd learned to trust my wife—and trust her a lot more than I trust myself. I had never gone wrong by trusting her. On the other hand, I had often gone wrong by trusting my own instincts, especially when it came to parenting. So I extended her a long line of credit on the unschooling question, and it has paid back the most generous dividends.

It turns out I was wrong about some of my hasty conclusions. Unschooling does *not* mean "no learning" or "no education," and certainly not "no parenting."

Nor does unschooling mean "no work." Some people dismiss it as laziness, because they think it requires less work. But that's not the case. It requires parents to be actively engaged in conversation and in relationship with each child, knowing each child's interests and cultivating those interests—and sharing those interests—even when we don't find the stuff interesting ourselves!

So you end up spending more time on it. The difference is that you're not working to satisfy somebody else's checklist or theory. You're working to make a home that fosters untrammeled learning. As parents, you're working to model an insatiable hunger for learning.

My wife pursued this in a gradual, instinctive way. She stored the TV away in a remote corner of the house, to be brought out only on occasion. Which meant it was a little arduous to watch TV, and the shows were never worth the effort. So we lost our taste for it, and when it stopped working we hardly noticed. I can't say any of us ever longed to have cable or a satellite dish.

God bless her. Not only did this save us money, it also extended our attention span—and made us turn to books for entertainment. We read books. We wrote books. Some of them got published.

Our kids grew up believing that reading, writing, and researching is what people do. I think more children should grow up with that belief. Believing will make it so. (Those who are philosophically inclined might think about unschooling in terms of virtue ethics.)

After decades of living this lifestyle, I'm ready to admit my wife was right. So is Suzie. I look at the adult children we've raised, and I find them wonderful. They're doing the work they love—and they're doing important work. They think for themselves, and they think good thoughts. I'm proud of them. I've always wanted my children to be prodigies of happiness, true happiness, and everything else is just lace around the edges. I think unschooling accomplishes that end—happiness—as well as anything I've seen.

I'm a great fan of the Victorian poet Coventry Patmore. Not long ago, I read an account, by one of his contemporaries, of the poet's education:

> Coventry was allowed in the main to educate himself by somewhat vague and desultory reading, varied by temporary incursions into mathematics, science, and art . . . It is indeed possible that the license was carried to undue lengths; and there are indications that Patmore took more than due advantage of the freedom accorded by a study insufficiently concentrated (Champneys, xviii-xix).

The biographer tsk-tsks that such an "unfettered educational career" took Patmore in some unfortunate directions. Indeed, his explorations led him to embrace the Christian faith at a very early age, and then to become a Roman Catholic. His inquiries went way outside the lines of Victorian propriety and led him to anticipate ideas that would, a century and a half later, find form as the Theology of the Body. His experiments made him one of the boldest poets of his day, profoundly influencing the work of Hopkins, Thompson, Tennyson, Carlyle, Ruskin, Browning, and the Pre-Raphaelites.

Not bad for life after a misspent childhood. I want my children to misspend days the same way.

But unschooling is not just good for my kids, it's good for me, too. I'm the breadwinner for a large family. That means I'm busy. I don't have time to spend mastering material, only to regurgitate it to my children till they can regurgitate it to me on a test. I've long since forgotten all the stuff I was forced to learn that way.

I do have time, though, to join the kids as they read and write, explore and discover. What's not to like about such a life?

Introduction

Write the vision;
make it plain upon tablets,
so he may run who reads it.

—Habakkuk 2:2

The naturalist Annie Dillard says in *The Writing Life*, "It takes years to write a book—between two and ten years." She also says, "It is the beginning of a work that the writer throws away."

I have to agree with her, twice. I started this book years ago—between two and ten, although closer to two—naively thinking I could get it to a publisher in six months and so to the reader in about a year. I see now that plan was unrealistic, but understandable because my first book, *Homeschooling with Gentleness*, followed a similar brief timeline. I was too wet behind the ears to see it would be tempting God to expect that kind of miracle again.

And so we come to my second sad realization: "It is the beginning of a work that the writer throws away" (*The Writing Life*, 5).

The problem is that when I began this book I had one particular thing in mind, but I continually entrusted my project to God, through the hands of St. Thérèse. She has handed me back a book that, while not entirely unlike the one I intended, is changed enough to make me throw out my first introduction. Not to mention the second, third, and fourth. This book, like a beloved child, grew under my nurturing influence and the protective blanket of my prayers, but like my own children it surprised me, becoming what God had in mind rather than what I had planned. I won't say that what it is now is anybody's guess. No, my job here is to tell you what the book is, and I am determined to do that, no matter how many attempts it takes.

My husband has tried to make my task easier, explaining—somehow surprised that I did not remember this, as we had learned it together in graduate school twenty years ago—that the purpose of an introduction is to render the reader benevolent, attentive, and docile. St. Thomas Aquinas is his source, we heard it first from Dr. McInerny, and I am in no position to argue with the three of them.

First, then, let me acquire your benevolence by telling you what this book will do for you.

At the outset, I planned a compilation of essays by Catholic unschoolers for Catholic unschoolers. If you are a Catholic unschooler, you will find compatriots here offering wisdom drawn from their experience.

Those of you who are not Catholic unschoolers will find something to help you as well. I mentioned that this book grew up according to God's plan, not mine; it grew up to be a book starring St. Thérèse of Lisieux, who refused to stay quietly in the subtitle. In the opening and closing chapters I offer you her unsurpassed, entirely sound, and marvelously hopeful doctrine of trustful surrender to God in all things. Her teaching alone is worth the price of the book, even if you are not sure about the unschooling part.

Having acquired your benevolence, next I am to get your attention. St. Thérèse and unschooling. Did that do it? The Little Way and John Holt. Are you intrigued? Appalled? Curious?

A problem is implicit in these pairs. I know all about it; it kept me up nights, until one day I decided to solve the problem for good. After two years of repeatedly asking my husband, "Are you sure we can unschool and be Catholic? Do you really think we can be Catholic and unschool?" I finally decided to write down his reassuring answers, his "Yes," and the reasons he gave. That was in May of 2003, and by June of 2004 *Homeschooling with Gentleness* was hot off the press.

The question that vexed me was the following: How could I, a faithful Catholic trying to raise healthy, holy children, find my educational method in the books of John Holt, who had no religious affiliation, no observable relationship with Christ, and actually said some pretty outrageous things occasionally? Granted I do not endorse everything John Holt wrote. I do not defend him on every point, nor try to canonize him, although I do pray for the repose of his soul. But why not find a more suitable mentor?

To put my dilemma another way, Seton Home Study rests on the respectable right of the Catholic homeschooling spectrum and Mother of Divine Grace sits solidly in the virtuous middle. Admirable faithful Catholics founded, run, and use them both. No one is compelling me to associate myself with the extreme left of this educational continuum. There are the Seton families constructively doing phonics workbooks, and classical homeschoolers agreeably attacking a list of phonemes with each child. Why am I over here in the LaLa-land of unstructured, unplanned unschooling, waiting for my son to notice the alphabet magnets on the fridge door? Does that make any sense, or is it irresponsible of me and unfair to my child? Why not move over to the unquestionably orthodox, structured, welcoming places farther to the right?

Strange as it seems, I gravitated to the informal leftish end of the homeschooling continuum at the beckoning of St. Thérèse. I even call unschooling a little way, with reference to hers. But let me clarify. I do not identify unschooling as *the* Little Way, nor do I think all Catholics should unschool.

I do consider the Little Way a useful model for us. We can imitate St. Thérèse and follow her example in seeking out the easy way to do things. She wrote in *Story of a Soul*:

> We are living now in an age of inventions, and we no longer have to take the trouble of climbing stairs, for, in the homes of the rich, an elevator has replaced these very successfully. I wanted to find an elevator which would raise me to Jesus, for I am too small to climb the rough stairway to perfection. (207)

I can honestly say that I am too small to climb the rough stairway that wends upward to the perfect education for my children. Instead of scaling the arduous heights of learning, we have taken the elevator of unschooling.

With your benevolence and attention secured, let me render you docile by reassuring you that in this book I provide a solution to the "Can a Catholic happily and sanely unschool?" question. I answer directly in the opening two chapters—first by considering St. Thérèse and unschooling, then by explaining that I see unschooling as a sensible practical approach to the mystery of learning, not as an ideology in competition with my faith.

Twelve more arguments for Catholic unschooling follow my chapters, arguments which are less direct, but possibly more compelling. In these essays my twelve co-authors highlight their struggles and successes with homeschooling, which have culminated in their adoption of some variation of unschooling.

You may well see your own life reflected in theirs, your challenges and victories, your exhaustion and elation. If you lean toward Catholic unschooling, you might identify more with the first eight women. If you are hesitant about it, and wondering how and why you would give up your desire for classical learning, or your penchant for Charlotte Mason's approach, wait until you meet the four women in Part Three. They have creatively combined unschooling principles with other educational methods that work well for their families.

Our Lord tells us, "Behold, I make all things new" (Revelation 21:5). May He use this book to do something new in your life. Whether you are a veteran homeschooler, just getting your feet wet, or happy with your children's schools, my contributors and I hope that *A Little Way of Homeschooling* brings to your home a share of the peace and respite that unschooling brings to ours.

Suzie Andres
October 1, 2010
Feast of St. Thérèse

How to Read This Book

I read a book twice as fast as anybody else. First I read the beginning, and then I read the ending, and then I start in the middle and read toward whichever end I like best.

—Gracie Allen

The purpose of this book is to aid homeschooling mothers, to remind them that God is on their side, and above all to make their lives easier.

I know your time is at a premium. There is an intrinsic order to the chapters, but that will be beside the point if you never get past Chapter 1. Please feel free to use this book in whatever way is most pleasant and helpful for you.

If you like to proceed methodically, start here and read straight through. It will probably take you two or three sittings to read the entire book. If you prefer, by all means skip around, reading what attracts you first.

Chapter 1, the Epilogue, and Appendix 1 feature the teachings of St. Thérèse, St. John Bosco, and St. Thomas Aquinas.

Chapters 3 through 15 are the ladies' essays, and taken together are like a day at the park with other moms. While the kids play, you can relax and get some much needed grown-up conversation. Just as at park day, every soul here is unique. You will find friends you relate to immediately, and others who remain mere smiling acquaintances.

We live according to plenty of rules, many necessary. In this book, there are no rules; read it however you like. Be yourself, follow your inclinations, and enjoy.

A Little Way of Homeschooling

PART ONE

Catholic Unschooling

CHAPTER ONE

St. Thérèse and Unschooling

At this time, Jesus was filled with gladness by the Holy Spirit, and said, "O Father, who are Lord of heaven and earth, I give you praise that you have hidden all this from the wise and the prudent, and revealed it to little children. Be it so, Lord, since this finds favour in your sight."

—Luke 10:21 (Knox)

"It is right and just to entrust oneself wholly to God and to believe absolutely what He says. It would be futile and false to place such faith in a creature" (§150). Thus the *Catechism of the Catholic Church* instructs us. And yet, how often have we placed our faith in men and human means, while doubting what God has told us? Jesus spoke plainly the night before He died, telling us, "Let not your hearts be troubled; believe in God, believe also in me. . . . Let not your hearts be troubled, neither let them be afraid" (John 14:1, 27). He was repeating during His last and most solemn sermon what He had already said many times during His life.

Not only at the end of His life, but also at the beginning, the admonition not to fear is Jesus' herald. The angel Gabriel reassures Mary, just prior to Jesus' conception in her womb, "Do not be afraid" (Luke 1:30). In the beginning of His public ministry, Jesus Himself explains that we only need to seek the Kingdom of God, and all the rest will be given to us. "Do not be anxious about tomorrow," He says, for "tomorrow will be anxious for itself" (Matthew 6:34). Later on He invites us to come to Him, to learn from Him because He will give us rest. He even promises "My yoke is easy, and my burden is light" (Matthew 11:30).

I remember a dear holy priest I used to know complaining that he did not find Jesus' yoke to be easy. I do not want to minimize the sufferings and trials and darkness that Jesus allows, perhaps even provides for us in His eternal wisdom. Nonetheless, whatever tomorrow and even later today may have in store, I do think we can begin at this moment to entrust ourselves and our families wholly to God, and believe absolutely what He says. He says we do not need to fear, we do not need to worry. We can come to Him and expect the work He gives us to be somehow easy and light.

St. Thérèse longed for this easy way, but she had to search for it. When she found it, she did all that she could to cling to it in her weakness, and she begged God to let her share her discovery. What was her treasure, her pearl of great price, her one thing necessary? She discovered that "Jesus does not demand great actions from us but simply *surrender* and *gratitude*" (*Story of a Soul*, 188), and then she applied herself to trusting Him and thanking Him. Thérèse was a realist, and knew there was work to be done, but she decided to do whatever came her way *without fear*, without worrying about the outcome, without the false notion that it depended on her.

Once during Thérèse's final illness, her sister Celine spoke to her about Thérèse's now impossible dream of going to Saigon to help found a Carmelite convent there. Celine suggested that when Thérèse was in Heaven she could send Celine in her place "to complete her work" and in this way the two together could do a perfect work. Thérèse responded:

> Ah, if you ever go over there, don't think it's to complete something. There is no need of this. Everything is good,

> everything is perfect, accomplished, it is love alone that counts. If you go there, this will be a whim of Jesus, nothing else. Don't think this would be a useful work, it would be a whim of Jesus. (*Last Conversations*, 262)

On an earlier occasion, when instructing the novices Thérèse had explained that they ought to be entirely detached from the work they were assigned. It is so easy to be distracted from our true purpose, our most important work, which is to love Jesus, to believe Jesus, to trust Jesus.

Those of us who are Catholic parents are often all too aware of the awesome work that God has given us. The *Catechism* teaches:

> The role of parents in education is of such importance that it is almost impossible to provide an adequate substitute. The right and the duty of parents to educate their children are primordial and inalienable. Parents must regard their children as children of God and respect them as human persons. Showing themselves obedient to the will of the Father in Heaven, they educate their children to fulfill God's law. (§2221-2222)

Clearly it is God's will for us to educate our children, to sow the seeds of His love in their lives, to provide them with the Sacraments, to teach them His ways, and start them off on their road to Heaven. If we have decided to homeschool, we add the entire burden of their intellectual formation to the spiritual and moral formation that is our first duty.

Before we get overwhelmed by the prospect of this enormous responsibility, let us turn again to St. Thérèse. She reassures us that we are not alone. Although Thérèse was not the mother of a family, she was placed in charge of the novices of her Carmel, and felt the task to be far beyond her abilities. Oh, how familiar the feeling! What mother has not sometimes wondered how God can be so reckless, entrusting these little souls to our care? But Thérèse found a solution. In *Story of a Soul* she writes:

> When I was given the office of entering into the sanctuary of souls, I saw immediately that the task was beyond my strength. I threw myself into the arms of God as a little child and, hiding my face in His hair, I said: 'Lord, I am too little to nourish Your children; if You wish to give through me what is suitable for each, fill my little hand and without leaving Your arms or turning my head, I shall give Your treasures to the soul who will come and ask for nourishment. . .' Mother, from the moment I understood that it was impossible for me to do anything by myself, the task you imposed upon me no longer appeared difficult. I felt that the only thing necessary was to unite myself more and more to Jesus and that 'all things will be given to you besides.' (*Last Conversations*, 237-238)

Like Thérèse, we need to find a solution for our inadequacy; our daily responsibilities await. She tells us, as she once told Celine, "Go to your *little duty*." But then Celine adds that Thérèse corrected herself, and said, "No, to your *little love*" (*Last Conversations*, 261).

What do we know as we go to our little duty, our little love? We know that if God has given us children, then He has given us the job of providing for their education. We know that we often feel burdened and even exhausted with this charge. And we know that "It is right and just to entrust oneself wholly to God and to believe absolutely what He says."

He says that His yoke (our work, done in union with Him) is easy, and His burden (which He shares with us in our daily duties) is light. How can we, alongside St. Thérèse, find a way to make our children's education light and easy? For us and for them? The purpose of this book is to introduce Catholic unschooling as a lighter and easier way to educate our children. For myself, and for the other contributors to this volume, unschooling has been a godsend.

There are many ways to educate our children, and I am firmly convinced that God intends there to be many ways. His creation is so varied that it would be a bizarre aberration if nature suddenly were, in this area of education, completely simple. God's perfections exist in Him simply, but we His creatures are limited, and so we express His beauty and goodness in manifold ways. Hence my first suggestion to parents is not "Unschool!" (which doesn't sound much like a suggestion), but rather, "Seek with St. Thérèse the easy way, the way that most comfortably fits your family. Believe Jesus and let His yoke be easy, His burden light."

Unschooling has been the easiest and most comfortable fit for my family. I knew it was right for us, because it was the educational approach that chased away my fear and spoke to me of love. I could really appreciate Thérèse's words when she wrote to her older sister in *Story of a Soul*, "No word of reproach touched me as much as did one of your caresses. My nature was such that fear made me recoil; with *love* not only did I advance, I actually *flew*" (174).

Then I heard an echo of her words when I read John Holt. John, like Thérèse, is articulate, sure, and passionate. He concludes the revised edition of *How Children Learn*:

> Little children love the world. That is why they are so good at learning about it. For it is love, not tricks and techniques of thought, that lies at the heart of all true learning. Can we bring ourselves to let children learn and grow through that love? (303)

He wrote, too, of fear in education, and how ineffective a tool it was. I thought of my own education, and agreed. He wrote of children's natural love of learning and desire to master the world around them. Again, I knew from experience that he was right.

But perhaps even more important than my conscious agreement with him, when I read John Holt I felt the same deep peace I felt when I read St. Thérèse. Their message to me has been essentially one and the same: Replace fear with trust. Since this is exactly what Jesus taught, I know it is good advice.

There are many beautiful aspects of unschooling, and many true principles that underlie its goodness. There are several excellent reasons to choose unschooling which you will read about in this book. But the truth, beauty, and goodness of unschooling are for me summed up in the words which were frequently spoken by John Holt, by St. Thérèse, and long before either, by Jesus. Trust. Do not fear.

If man were not rational, a learning animal; if what children needed to learn was very complicated and far beyond their abilities; if there were some urgent rush or severely limited time frame in which children had to learn all they needed for this life and the next; or if the family could not provide a safe environment in which the child could explore and gain access to the world at a modest pace . . . then maybe unschooling would be a bad idea. But darned if those children in Japan do not learn Japanese before they are even four years old. And I do not see why children don't actually have about sixteen or eighteen years to prepare for further education, or training, or life outside the home. Finally, I have every confidence that in normal circumstances the family can offer the best possible nurturing haven for a child. But it is all much simpler than this for me. Trust, don't fear. My yoke is easy, my burden light.

Which brings us back to St. Thérèse. She surprised her sister Celine one day. They were standing in front of a library and she said, "Oh, I would have been sorry to have read all those books!" Celine wondered why and pointed out, "This would have been quite an acquisition. I would understand your regretting to read them, but not to have already read them." Thérèse had a different way of looking at it, saying, "If I had read them, I would have broken my head, and I would have wasted precious time that I could have employed very simply in loving God" (*Last Conversations*, 261).

I think one of our methods for multiplying worries is telling ourselves that our job in educating our children is to do our best, to get them to do their best, and to pack as much knowledge and wisdom into them as is possible. How much more profitable for us to begin from Thérèse's reminder, "It's only in Heaven that we'll see the whole truth about everything. This is impossible on earth" (*Last Conversations*, 132).

God will give each of us the time that we need to learn everything He wants us to know; this applies to both ourselves and our children. Why do we expect that we must teach it all to our children in our homeschool? And why do we automatically assume that this burden of prospective learning will be painful for them, arduous for us? There is a much less frightening way.

The goal I am setting before you is to seek out a way to pursue learning with pleasure and freedom. In the spirit of St. Thérèse, we as Catholics ought to realize that Jesus has set us free. If we believe His words, if we strive to believe Him more and more, we will start by living one day at a time, letting tomorrow take care of itself. Already we will have made progress if we refuse to see the whole future of a child contained in today's accomplishments, successes, and failures.

Let us follow Thérèse along her Little Way. Let us trust Jesus and believe His words. Let us be confident that He who is Truth, who can neither deceive nor be deceived, will fulfill every promise He has made.

We need to ask Our Lord to show us the particular way He has laid out for each of us. As Thérèse explains: "Jesus has no need of books or teachers to instruct souls; He teaches without the noise of words. Never have I heard Him speak, but I feel that He is within me at each moment: He is guiding and inspiring me with what I must say and do" (*Story of a Soul*, 179).

Spend time listening to Him, and let Him tell you what He desires for you and your family. It may be unschooling, it may be a formal homeschooling program, it may be something entirely different. Whatever it is, you will recognize it by the peace it brings to you and your children. Do not settle for anything less.

CHAPTER TWO

Is Unschooling an Ideology?

This is the property of love: to seek out all the good things of the Beloved.

—St. John of the Cross
The Living Flame of Love

I have always admired people with strong opinions and those whose lives seem to center around one main idea or mission. Figures such as St. Thérèse of Lisieux, Jerome Lejeune, Conrad Baars, Isabel Myers and Katherine Briggs, and in the field of education, Charlotte Mason, Maria Montessori, and John Holt come to mind. It seems to me so noble, such a sign of integrity to live one's life dedicated to an ideal, pursuing the good and intent on sharing it with others.

One trait these people have in common, and which I want to emulate, is a deep philosophical bent characterized by wonder, introspection, strong powers of observation, and a clear insight into the nature of things. Although, as far as I can tell, some of my heroes have not known the light of Christ in this life, I nevertheless learn from them with great joy, remembering the words of St. Thomas, "All truth, by whomever spoken, comes from the Holy Spirit" (*On Truth*, q. 1, a. 8). Beyond their knowledge of the truth, what I most appreciate in these men and women is their love of the truth, and the dedication they had to living, speaking, and spreading the truth at every opportunity.

Despite my best attempts, my own enthusiasms never actually translate into a mission. Thus I must admit that although I have become something of an expert on Catholic unschooling, to my chagrin I do not preach it exclusively, nor do I recommend it to everyone. Even in my own home, I have been known to swing wildly between my unschooling leanings and the lure of boarding school. I am not always sure that unschooling is the best way, and that stops me from being an apostle and evangelist of unschooling. What's my problem? Am I unconvinced, uncommitted, or merely timid? All of these possibilities have crossed my mind, but I think there is a deeper reason for my lack of single-mindedness. Unschooling, as I see it, is not an ideology, and that is one thing that stops me from being its doctrinaire champion.

John Holt, the man who coined the term "unschooling," was an educator and educational reformer who eventually gave up on schools. He was a teacher in the 1950s and '60s, a writer in the 1960s and '70s, and finally a supporter of parents who wanted to teach their children at home in the 1970s and early '80s. John died of cancer in 1985, but colleagues, friends, and followers carried on his work in education. Unschooling became the movement dedicated to promoting the child's initiative in learning by eschewing schools and formal academics. As John Holt noted, children are learning all the time and unschoolers allow this to go on at the child's own pace, in his own way, with minimal interference from the adults in charge. Many unschooling proponents are adamant about some aspect of this learning process, but still I maintain that unschooling is not an ideology.

Why not? Because Holt himself, who is the clearest exponent of this educational attitude, was not an ideologue. He was a great observer of human nature, but to be more exact, a great observer of particular human beings. Holt observed children, seeking to understand how they learned, how their interactions with adults affected their learning, and what adults could do—or ought not do—to best facilitate this learning.

He was the man who showed me what children are like. At the time I first read his books, I had a ten-year-old son with whom I spent the majority of my days. I knew something about this boy, but it was John's clear writing, his love for children, and his careful observations which opened my eyes to the child before me and made sense of my experience with him.

Reading John's books made me eager to become a naturalist with him, one who "is a good noticer," in the words of Dr. Dolittle's parrot Polynesia. John helped me to appreciate the mystery and beauty of children and made me want to spend time with them. Most of all, I learned from his words and example that unschooling, like every type of childhood education, must be for the sake of the children. Furthermore, no benefit will come from clinging tightly to theories about the child's nature and what is best for him if we lose sight of the child himself. As John wrote in *How Children Learn*:

> My aim in writing is not primarily to persuade educators and psychologists to swap new doctrines for old, but to persuade them to *look* at children, patiently, repeatedly, respectfully, and to hold off making theories and judgments about them until they have . . . a reasonably accurate model of what children are like. (271)

In other words, unschooling makes much more sense when we think of it as a suggestion rather than a mandate. Be with the children. Really look at them. Enjoy spending time together, talking, investigating, reading, playing. If you can wait and see, you will discover that they learn so much, so often, in such entirely individual ways.

When my older son Joseph began learning to write, I thought that I needed to show him the correct way. The book we were using had arrows next to each letter. It started with A and went through to Z, and on each page the workbook guided the child to write the letter the one correct way. Start here, go this direction, don't lift your pencil, move around to the bottom, and so on. With my careful help, Joseph began to hate writing. What began as a pleasure—learning to write, to express himself just like a grown-up—quickly became a way to make mistakes, be corrected, remain unable.

Now when people ask what I do for school with Dominic, my younger son, I don't have much to say. I mostly let him go, and then I enjoy the results. I answer his questions which, like the questions of other children, often have to do with reading, writing, and arithmetic. Sometimes they are about religion, science, or history. In his own way, at his own pace, he is learning what he wants to know. There are no big surprises. It turns out that he wants to know what people have always wanted to know: how to communicate, verbally and in written form; how to understand other people's communications, especially the written ones; what numbers do and how they work; and on and on.

When he does a "math problem" and it looks like nothing I have ever seen, I need him to explain. Oh, it's written backward and practically upside down, and the answer is wrong. In fact, at first glance it seems to be mostly mistakes. Then I see that our little boy has figured out how equations are written, he has worked on his own question of 12 + 12, he has used his fingers to count beyond 10, and he almost got it right. Looked at in this light, his work is truly amazing. Yes he got it wrong, but that often matters to him as well as to us, and of his own accord he will keep at it until he sorts it out.

John Holt spent a lot of time observing children. I have spent a considerable amount of time doing this as well. Am I ready to adopt and propose a theory or judgment? To some extent, yes. I am convinced that unschooling is a wonderful, workable approach to education. I am almost always certain it is the way for us.

And when I hear that a good Catholic school is adding on a first-grade Montessori classroom five minutes from my home, what is my reaction? I spend two sleepless nights and two investigative days considering whether this new option would fit us better than unschooling. A friend counsels me that making the decision to send this child to this school for this year can be considered unschooling, if we are thinking of unschooling as being attentive to the needs of the child and responding accordingly. I think I agree with her, and yet I wonder . . . Can schooling really be unschooling? And on the other hand, why can't I just be doctrinaire?

My son Joseph, bearing the privileges that come with being eighteen, is doctrinaire. I do not begrudge him this. If we weren't idealistic and sure of ourselves at eighteen, what chance would we have against the slings and arrows the future holds? In this case, he is sure the school thing is a bad idea.

In fact, when I think of Catholic unschooling, I think of Joseph. He is The Catholic Unschooler. When asked at the end of his high-school years whether he would like to participate in a local Catholic homeschool graduation ceremony, Joseph responded, "No. I'd be glad to help my friends celebrate. They've finished their work, they've been working hard at school. But me? What would I be graduating from? Life?" And when he heard his dad and me whispering and spelling about the M-o-n-t-e-s-s-o-r-i S-c-h-o-o-l for his brother, he was aghast. "You scoundrel!" he laughed at me, "and right when you're working on this book!"

Why is Joseph so convinced that unschooling is the way to go? He has his own experience of school lurking in the depths of his memory (two fairly happy years when he was four and five), the shadow of my attempts to teach him things in our early years of homeschooling, and then the experience of a decade or so of fairly broad freedom to learn in his own way. He used that time well, though I hasten to add that he is not a genius, nor has he ever been a model of self-discipline. When I waver in my fidelity to unschooling, Joseph is usually around to remind me of its virtues.

As I look back over the years, I am encouraged and inspired by our family's progress in learning and convinced again of the practical truths embodied in the unschooling approach. In hindsight I realize that almost as soon as I became aware that what we were doing was unschooling, I was put to the test. Joseph was entering his high-school years. Were we serious about this seemingly unserious approach? What about his preparation for college? What about the transcript that would be required in four years? I knew what I needed to do. I needed to commit myself to doing nothing.

My thinking was this: If I tried to keep track of Joseph's activities, reading, and all the rest, I would be tempted to turn everything into a recordable moment, and push every interest into some significant learning experience. In other words, the learning we had come to terms with as natural and often spontaneous would in the interest of documentation likely become artificial and forced. At the least I would make my life miserable by feeding my fear, wondering, *Is he doing enough?* In the worst case scenario I would drive Joseph crazy and deaden his desire to learn by requiring constant reports on his learning. Once again I looked to my husband for reassurance, and we decided not to worry about anything.

Four years later we have survived to tell the tale, and the good news is that it actually worked. Each year Tony, Joseph, and I considered what academic work was important at that stage, and we kept it to a minimum. Joseph's interests continued to develop, and he found new ways to explore what fascinated him. His study of piano bore fruit in original compositions; his interest in fantasy inspired him to begin a science fiction novel; his love of weaponry and warfare led him into the sports of paintball, airsoft, and roller hockey. His reflections on his own education found validation in the writings of John Taylor Gatto, the award-winning New York teacher who publicly renounced the school system and writes about its inherent problems. His appetite for good literature found satiety in the writings of Chesterton, Belloc, Tolkien, and Lewis, among others.

Now my family has entered the next stage of our lives, with Joseph leaving home to enter college. Since our older son is living outside the home, the focus is on Dominic. Somehow it never occurred to me before, but it turns out that if your children are born twelve years apart, you will graduate one (with or without ceremony) just in time for the next to start formal schooling. In our case, because we unschool, Dominic's life will not change dramatically now that he is "in first grade." Unless, of course, I succumb to the recurrent temptation of enrolling him in school.

Even as I reflect on what I consider the success of our unschooling experiment with Joseph, another part of my mind is busy considering options for Dominic's education. Sometimes I wonder whether I will ever feel wholeheartedly committed to anything. And then I remember: I am entirely committed to the Church, to my husband, and to doing my best for our children. But I am blessed with the ability to see good in many places, and this can make life confusing.

Often I find that what appeals to me about sending Dominic to school is not an image of what he will be doing there, but an image of what I will be doing while he is there. My eighteen-year-old is moving out, and the only thing standing between me and all the activities I would like to pursue is a six-year-old with a personality the size of a house. When it comes down to it, I think that every mother who homeschools is heroic. Parenting has always been a self-sacrificing profession; add in homeschooling and you reach a whole new level. The problem for me comes when I start to think of that new level as martyrdom. Granted, compared to most Catholic mothers I know, I have it pretty easy. And yet, there is that pull—if Dominic were in school, I could . . .

Then I remember. When Joseph was born, I held him in my arms and thought *Wow, I will never be lonely again*. When I found out I was expecting Dominic, I said, "Now I know what I will be doing for the next eighteen years." I chose marriage hoping God would bless us with children, and He has. I chose homeschooling partly because I did not want to miss a single moment with them.

In everyday life, it turns out there are many moments with my children that I would be glad to miss. My experience has shown me that two things are true about time and children. First, children grow up really fast, and before you know it they are grown and gone. Second, if you homeschool, every day seems like a whole day with lots of hours and even more minutes and an interminable number of seconds. For me, then, mothering is a balancing act between time with the children and time snatched alone; if I can get some of both, I'm a happier camper. But at the end of that very long day, our homeschooling is still a choice. It helps me to keep making that choice, and to consider other options when they arise. I want to know and remind myself that my family has chosen unschooling because it is a path of freedom. When I stop feeling free, which happens, I can reconsider and make sure it is still a path of freedom.

When I feel troubled with this frequent re-evaluation, and wish for a little more stability, I can ask myself again, "What's wrong with rigid adherence to a fixed system?" The answer I come up with is that adherence to truth is not a problem. A fixed system, however, is a little too contrived. In graduate school, Dr. McInerny used to make the same point about the study of St. Thomas. Many people see Thomism as a system of thought, but in doing so they lose its grounding in reality and experience. Our teacher insisted that the better approach was to learn from St. Thomas. He does have a doctrine, and we can be his disciples, but that is quite different from being adherents to a system.

And so I return again to the truths implied by unschooling, rather than sticking merely to an ideology. Whenever I look into a particular school, and this new one turns out to be no exception, I am brought back to the principles that we live in unschooling. Let the child learn by his own initiative, in his own way. The basics are not hard, children want to learn them, and they will ask for help when they need it. Learning is easiest and most effective when it is spontaneous and entered into by desire. Our home life will include necessary tasks, obligations, and duties, but learning does not have to be one of them.

I wonder how John Holt could be single-minded without becoming driven or ideological. I do not know the answer to that, but I admire him for it. Like him, I hope always to love children, to be a reverent observer of the mystery of learning, and to be an advocate of unschooling. If I must do this amid my own frequent questioning, I can live with that. I am grateful to have found the principles and truth that support unschooling, and I can be content with falling short of my ideal. I will probably never be a woman with a mission. Instead I am content to be a woman with children, happily unschooling for the moment.

PART TWO

Catholic Unschoolers

CHAPTER THREE

Cindy's Family: Learning in Freedom and Faith

Cindy Kelly was raised in the Bible Belt, married a cradle Catholic, and discovered the truth and beauty of the Faith, converting twelve years ago. She and John, her husband of twenty-four years, are the parents of two sons aged fourteen and seventeen. They live in Texas and have homeschooled since their oldest boy was in kindergarten; their second son is a "preschool dropout" who has never looked back. Cindy works from home, as a Program Advisor for College Plus!, and is an Account Manager for Lighthouse Catholic Media, an evangelical apostolate. She and her sons also operate a small pet-sitting business for fun and spending money. You can find Cindy on facebook at cinkel3@swbell.net and blogging at http://cindykellyfamily.blogspot.com/.

Trust children.
Nothing could be more simple,
or more difficult.

—John Holt, *How Children Learn*

When I began homeschooling I thought I was doing so to give my then six-year-old son a better education. I was wrong; I was not just giving him a better education, I was giving him a better life.

My son started his school career in an award-winning, state of the art kindergarten, but before the first semester passed, I knew something was amiss. He was losing his sense of wonder. An intelligent, creative child, he had become compliant and bored. Fun activities he used to love had turned into chores. I volunteered in the classroom and saw the children spending an inordinate amount of time getting herded into lines and earning stickers for being quiet. My heart told me this was not the right path for us. Furthermore, our home life was changing. Our days of being together and exploring were dominated by the schedule of that little kindergarten, and his best hours of the day were given to school.

In the midst of this, I stumbled upon the seemingly radical concept of homeschooling, and we decided to give it a try. It was a difficult decision to make since my friends were without exception ferrying their children down the public school route. I had no idea what lay in store, how my vision of education would be transformed, how our Faith would so beautifully intertwine with life and learning. Nearly a dozen years later, I realize I was seeking a freer childhood for my son, a childhood enjoyed outside of the boxes imposed by a traditional school.

Like many of my generation, I had always intended to send my children to public school. It was what one did, being oneself a product of the system. I now see the irony of my former position, since my own strongest schoolgirl memories were not my favorite ones. There was scarce one-on-one time with the teacher and simply no opportunity to delve into those things which aroused our curiosity. Instead we spent our time waiting—waiting for the teacher to pass out papers, for others to finish their work, or for the disruptive kids to settle down. I would sit, bored, listening to the teacher drone on with instructions I had understood long before, hoping the bell would ring so I could go play with my friends. My most creative hours were spent at home doing projects, playing in the neighborhood, learning oil painting from a friend's mom and horseback riding on their family farm.

In contrast to the usual school tedium, I remember a small bright spot in junior high. I was working independently on a geography project in a seminar room—I was actually learning, and full of joy! Suddenly the bell rang, ending class before I could finish. The teacher smiled understandingly, shrugged her shoulders, and directed me on to my next assigned class. I felt let down, and even betrayed. The bright spot dimmed. I sensed it was not the teacher who had failed me, but the system, the whole environment of the school. This experience reinforced the subtle lesson that I should work for grades, but not invest too much of myself in my education.

Fast forward to a class I took in graduate school. The professor would assign us a gargantuan amount of reading, then every Tuesday and Thursday we would meet to talk about it. The eight of us (one teacher and seven students) sat around a conference table sipping Coke, and discussed the texts. It was heaven, one of my first experiences of genuine learning in a seventeen year career of formal schooling.

What made the difference? Ideas. That professor allowed and encouraged us to talk about ideas. He wanted to hear what we thought. The readings were there to give us the background and springboard for discussion, but the goal was to share and think and really learn.

The question then arises: Isn't there a way our children can encounter such learning while still in their childhood? Must they wait until graduate school? And what if they don't make it that far through the system? Children are born with minds that are eager to investigate the world. Often by third or fourth grade their bright enthusiasm to learn has faded, and passivity has taken its place. Hopefully, by adulthood we all have known moments when learning was spontaneous, when we naturally made connections, when we were inspired to follow up on something that intrigued us. Must these moments be postponed or sacrificed altogether in the name of education?

Reflecting on that college class, I see that learning depends upon our relationships, the relationships we have with ideas and with each other. Unfortunately, school had for the most part closed my mind to ideas, and I had to consciously work to recover my original childhood sense of wonder. As we began homeschooling, I knew that I wanted to give the gift of real learning to my children, but it was difficult to know how to proceed. Because it was what I had experienced, the traditional school method was all I knew.

True to form as a first year homeschooling mom, I threw myself into researching curriculum. With great gusto I planned out the school year for our two young sons. I used the most gentle and appealing programs I could find, but I imposed a schedule that soon caused serious difficulty in our home. I was not sure of my role. Was I mom, teacher, or drill sergeant? Providence intervened, through a friend who introduced me to Charlotte Mason's approach to education. I raced through *For the Children's Sake* by Susan Schaeffer McCauley and *A Charlotte Mason Companion* by Karen Andreola. These two books convincingly portrayed the beauty and joy of learning with children.

As I read, I was brought back to the ambiance of my graduate school economics class. There was *more* to the acquisition of knowledge than just learning facts, more than using canned curriculum and staying on track with scope and sequence. There was a way to encourage wonder and thought, and we were ready for it. Thanks to this nineteenth-century educator, I caught my first glimpse of the happiness that homeschooling can bring. This happiness was beyond the satisfaction of doing as well as or better than the brick-and-mortar schools; this was about learning as a lifetime pursuit.

In *A Charlotte Mason Companion*, Karen Andreola captured the essence of giving our children the world of wonder of ideas when she said: "Be sure that your children each day have: Something or someone to love, Something to do, Something to think about" (24). Karen summed up beautifully Miss Mason's teaching that if we respect our children as "born persons" and provide for them a feast of ideas within a rich atmosphere, they will thrive. Karen and Charlotte propose not only a rich physical atmosphere with "living books," access to nature and crafts aplenty, but also a rich emotional atmosphere, where children are encouraged to ask questions and are validated in their plans and passions. Charlotte knew we could trust children to make connections and learn.

As the years went on, we enjoyed what we gleaned from Charlotte and I owe a debt of gratitude to her. She proposed a set of ideals I believe in, for they are rooted in the awareness that God created each of us as a unique human being. She gave me permission to toss boring curriculum. More importantly, her writings gave me the confidence I lacked in leaving behind the traditional school setting. Her approach enabled us to adopt a method that was still legitimate in the world's eyes, but which freed us to begin discovering our own distinctive learning style.

To this day we appreciate much of Charlotte Mason's wisdom. She knew how subjects overlap, intertwine, and connect, and for this reason she called learning the "Science of Relations." We have retained her understanding, while giving up the subject divisions and schedules that she needed in her schools. While Charlotte was still a classroom teacher (albeit a sensitive and dynamic one), we live in the freedom of our home. Here we have seen everyday life and learning become more of an organic process which somewhat defies description because it is seamless and all encompassing.

As I continued my research on children and how they learn, it was nearly inevitable that I would find John Holt. This beloved man adored children; he understood and respected them. I have often thought it would be such fun to host a dinner party and introduce Miss Mason to Mr. Holt! I think they would be kindred spirits, each a reformer in his own time who labored purely for the children's sake.

Holt, a highly respected teacher, attempted repeatedly to reform the American school system in the 1960s. He saw how it was stifling learning, disrespecting children, and squelching their natural desire to know. He did his best to work within the system to effect serious change, but after years of being thwarted, he finally gave up. He believed his attempts to change the school system had been useless, but in fact his writing had attracted attention. Slowly a following of parents similarly disillusioned with school gathered around him.

Holt knew that children could be trusted to learn without all the structure, curriculum, and hours behind desks that were the norm. With his encouragement, and the help of his newsletter *Growing Without Schooling*, parents began teaching their children at home. He wrote in his book *How Children Learn*:

> The child is curious. He wants to make sense out of things, find out how things work, gain competence and control over himself and his environment, and do what he can see other people doing. He is open, perceptive, and experimental. He does not merely observe the world around him, he does not shut himself off from the strange, complicated world around him, but tastes it, touches it, hefts it, bends it, breaks it. To find out how reality works, he works on it. He is bold. He is not afraid of making mistakes. And he is patient. He can tolerate an extraordinary amount of uncertainty, confusion, ignorance, and suspense . . . . School is not a place that gives much time, or opportunity, or reward, for this kind of thinking and learning. (287)

And again, in *Learning All the Time* Holt says:

> A child only pours herself into a little funnel or into a little box when she's afraid of the world—when she's been defeated. But when a child is doing something she's passionately interested in, she grows like a tree—in all directions. (156)

John Holt's notions caught on and became known as unschooling. He showed how schoolish techniques are not needed for a child to learn, and often they actually impede learning. I don't think of unschooling as equivalent to unparenting or unlearning. To the contrary, the facets of unschooling we have adopted in our home have required megaparenting and superlearning. Unschooling has granted us the liberty both to let go of techniques that don't work for us and also to embrace the tools that do. The result has been much more than a 183-day school year could ever provide.

As I gave up traditional curricula and the associated researching, planning, and implementing of it, I noticed that a vacuum of time emerged for my two boys and myself. Slowly and steadily this vacuum was filled with concerns and activities. At first the journey was rough, as my sons kept waiting for the honeymoon to be over and the lessons to start up again. It was as if they were waiting for the other shoe to drop—for me to once again wield my Excel spreadsheet schedules. But I restrained myself, time passed, and they began to trust.

They began to send down taproots. No longer did they run when they saw me coming, thinking another lesson was on the way or afraid that I would ruin a burgeoning interest with a teachable-moment-turned-assignment. Instead I started simply to share with them what I found intriguing, allowing them to take or leave the information.

When the boys realized there were no strings attached, they became increasingly accepting of new ideas. I had time to pursue my own enthusiasms, and naturally I shared these with the boys, many of which they adopted as their own. Our unschooling allowed them to observe my enjoyment of learning, which was very encouraging to them. My sons liked seeing me absorbed in my projects, and they would often check on me and support me in my efforts.

My husband, who was not overly involved in our previous formal curriculum, was more easily able to join in. He began to offer more and more of his insights into history and the Faith, and the boys took this offering for what it was: not a lesson, but an opportunity to learn about their dad's viewpoint and passions.

As my husband and I modeled following our interests, this behavior rubbed off on the boys. They gained confidence in their ability to find the truth they need, and equally important, they came to realize that they do not, and could not possibly, know everything. There will always be holes in our education and a lifetime to fill them. We discovered that learning is an incredibly fun and fulfilling experience, not another chore on a to-do-list. The mood of the house changed, and it became a livelier place.

Much of my time now is spent finding avenues to explore together. I am ever on the lookout, ready to employ any resource that seems to fit us, including texts, online classes, discussion groups, and occasionally curriculum. Knowledge comes in many forms, and I have found that I need to keep my mind alert to every possibility. I also have come to recognize that all learning counts, even if I wasn't the one to research or plan it! In fact, it is often most meaningful to my sons if they discover it on their own.

One great vehicle to learning is conversation, something I believe is vastly underrated today. Charlotte Mason employed a technique called narration, in which a child, having read or otherwise gained information, would then "tell it back." This process allows children to take in ideas, think them through, and make them their own through retelling. Charlotte used this in lieu of tests, for it gave her a good indication of where her students were academically, as well as giving them practice thinking. Narration is a precursor to formal composition.

Conversation is really doing the same thing as narration, but in a more natural way. I am constantly in awe as I listen to my sons tell back their thoughts about what they have learned, and the connections they have made. Along these lines, one of my great pleasures is hearing the boys talk with their friends. They cover a wide range of subjects: politics, video games, faith, sports, and philosophy. In these conversations they are not only exchanging opinions, but also learning how to tolerate views that are different from their own.

While the unschooling approach as we practice it may sound simple, I don't want to make light of the inherent difficulty it involves: namely, it requires us to give up the school mentality that dominates society. But since we have lived this life, and I have reflected on what we have learned and how we have learned, I see that it works.

There are some basics that I hope for my children. These include a love of reading and writing; math, science, and history literacy; and a good understanding of our Faith. I keep little lists and lots of journals. If I see we need bolstering in an area, I find living resources to fit us and introduce them either informally or sometimes a little more energetically. I have found that a vacuum can provide a lot of room for growth, and filling the vacuum has been a labor of love for me. The most powerful way to encourage my sons to enjoy a new area of learning is to model it myself and continue our dialogue about their interests and mine.

Every so often I will take one or the other son to our local coffee shop, buy him a latte, and talk with him about life—his world and the world out there, and what God may be telling him about it today. Where will he fit in? What will God's plan for him be? Has he had any insights since our last chat?

On a regular basis we talk about the boys' current fascinations, what they are doing, new interests they might like to pursue, and what I can do to help. As they have grown older, we have discussed what education is. We talk about Charlotte Mason and John Holt, we explore what learning is and the many relationships involved in it.

I address areas I think they might look into to achieve their goals, or that might be engaging to them. For example, one son is getting close to college age, but is not sure what he wants to do. We know his strengths, and that helps us talk in generalities about possible careers. We talk about getting ready for college, and how that could be done. But we also know areas in which he has no interest, so we don't waste time on those. We talk about the importance of knowing oneself, listening to God, and taking initiative in coming up with one's own plan.

A concept that has been helpful in the college and work conversations has been that of "tickets." Tickets are the things that open doors to that next level: a high-school transcript, an SAT score, or a foreign language credit. Though we are primarily non-traditional learners, we are aware that the rest of the world lives by rules and parameters. To reach goals, we have to understand how to translate our learning into the world's terms (which we are doing with simple transcripts) and be willing to meet benchmarks which colleges or employers set.

I think these conversations have been invaluable. When I was a teenager and in college, I only knew one thing: how to play the game. I knew that if I got A's and pleased professors, I would advance, and I did. I wish I had known that while it is fine to play the game, the game is not the goal. The goal is finding God's will for me and my place in the world. College and work are intermediate goals when they allow me to follow the path God has laid out for me. And those tickets that get me where I need to be are nothing more than steppingstones. Finally, I wish I had known that throughout the whole process, authentic learning can be had.

We have used curricula on and off in the past, and, as I've mentioned, in our early homeschooling days it was not a positive experience. I cannot honestly blame the curricula. What was amiss was my relationship to it and the role I allowed it to play in my house. When introducing a curriculum, I had already invested a great deal of time and money in it. Moreover, I had invested my credibility in it, and I did not want to admit—especially to my children—that I had made a mistake in choosing it. The consequence was that the curriculum no longer seemed to be a means, but became the end itself. It became our master, and disordered our relationships with each other and with learning.

On the other hand, when kept in its proper role as our servant, curricula have served us very well. When we want to form a bedrock of information upon which we can build, it is great. For example, when my boys were young, we used the *Baltimore Catechism* and books in the Faith and Life series. We have profited from math curricula, science texts and DVDs, and in general, from resources in which information was presented succinctly.

The key was to have a goal for the curriculum. I needed to know what we were trying to learn and why. Were we aiming at content or skill-building or both? A recent online writing course offers a perfect example of curriculum that is providing both content (how to write a college essay) and skill-building (how to relate to teachers and negotiate a syllabus and course of study). Our fourteen-year-old son got an A in this school-type course, although he had little prior experience with formal writing curricula. We spoke about the expectations, and he took it from there. He learned how to play the game, which in this case meant following the instructor's rules. His success was a wonderful confirmation of our unschooling. It turned out that his nontraditional life had prepared him well for traditional requirements, and when this opportunity arose, he was ready to make full use of it.

Having discovered the true role of curricula, I no longer fear its tyrannical rule. When I look at my boys, I have stopped imagining a long list of subjects I must load upon them; I do not worry about finding programs for each, and then having our success depend on how well we implement them. Now I see any curriculum as just another tool. It is not more important than museum visits, conversations, or living books, and it must suit the child at the time.

When we get down to it, what is the real purpose of education? What is the reason for learning about our world and the people in it? We will settle for no less than love and truth, ultimately found in Christ Himself. All worthy roads lead to Christ and the Church, and if we can help lead our children to this goal, we have done well.

Having our children at home gives us a tremendous opportunity. We can spread out the feast of ideas, interact, build trusting relationships, and foster communication. We can lay the framework for faith in a sacramental life, read the *Catechism*, study Scripture. As we have talked about bugs in the dirt with our toddlers, the latest advances in science with our adolescents, and finally critical political elections with our nearly grown sons, we have been able, naturally and honestly, to bring these topics back to God's creation and our Catholic Faith. This is Catholic unschooling for our family.

These years with our children are such a gift. Building relationships requires sacrifice, and sometimes we may think it would be easier to simply drop the kids off at school, or buy a packaged curriculum and forget the rest. But then we realize the beauty that surrounds us. Walking with our children, helping them encounter the delights of learning and living out the truths of our Faith, these have spelled joy for us. We have grown not only by breaking out of the traditional school curriculum mode, but also by discovering our interests and personalities and passions. We are becoming who we are as a family in Christ.

CHAPTER FOUR

Amy's Family: A Return to Unschooling

Amy and Michael Wagner are the parents of six children aged eleven to twenty-two. Amy attended universities in Colorado, Oregon, and Hawaii, majoring in fine arts; she was confirmed a Catholic at age thirty-two. Her husband Michael, a Navy man and lifelong Catholic, earned his bachelor's degree from a distance university while defending our country. Now a master electrician, he works for the railroad. The Wagners live in Colorado and have been homeschooling for eighteen years.

Families, be who you are!

—Pope John Paul II, *Familiaris Consortio*

From the beginning, discussions with and written reflections by homeschooling friends have helped me to appreciate that each family is unique, and mine is no exception. I am finally taking to heart Pope John Paul II's admonition, *Families, be who you are!*

My family consists of my husband and me, and our six children aged eleven to twenty-two. Our homeschooling journey has come full circle, and after all these years I am at last finding the courage to let us live the unschooling life.

Here is where we started: unschooling. I subscribed for several years to John Holt's newsletter *Growing Without Schooling*, even before my first child was school age. Just about everything in it resonated with me; it depicted life as I wished I could have lived it growing up. It was what I wanted for my own children. My husband was with me in believing what I was doing was right, and that was good.

Now, about fifteen years later, here is where we have ended up: unschooling. A life without school, yet learning all the time. In between then and now, however, there were about ten years of school-at-home homeschooling, which at one point meant six children scattered throughout grades one to twelve working through a formal curriculum. Why the detour? Our journey went something like this . . .

When our first child reached the magical age of six, that is, school age, my husband and I needed to seriously consider what we would do for his education. I was already familiar with the idea of homeschooling through my acquaintance with *Growing Without Schooling*, and furthermore, a good friend had started teaching her children at home.

Homeschooling looked attractive because I really liked this woman and her kids. Also, having recently received the sacrament of Confirmation, I was gradually becoming aware of the shortcomings of Catholic parochial schools. My husband and I were growing by leaps and bounds in our knowledge and love for the Faith, through reading various Catholic catechisms and encyclicals with a small group of adults. It bothered us that in most cases the parochial schools seemed to be giving up their Catholic identity, abandoning a Catholic curriculum for secular textbooks. In any event, we realized that we couldn't afford Catholic school tuition unless we nixed traveling and family vacations.

Tuition fees and secularism aside, the primary reason I wanted to school our children at home was related to my own early years, during which I was bussed from a rural area to a small town school. These bus rides were a sore affliction, with much abusive behavior directed at me and no help offered by the driver. It didn't occur to me to tell my parents what I suffered on those bus rides. I assumed nothing could be done, since taking the bus was the only way to get to school. Depressing, I agree! But it taught me this, that masses of children in close proximity are more likely to act like the characters in *Lord of the Flies* than not.

In 1991 we officially started homeschooling. I shuddered at the thought of the paperwork and reporting required by the most popular of the Catholic homeschool programs, and so we used a local umbrella school with a supportive and very "unschooly" director. And so our family began our homeschool journey with a freewheeling program. I barely planned ahead. I had no notion of scope and sequence, or of finishing certain books in a school year. My sons' interests determined our direction, in large part. I read aloud to them from books I thought worthwhile, and they chose many as well. We progressed through learning to read, write, and do basic arithmetic. In short, we went our merry little way.

When my firstborn took his own time learning to read, I was not alarmed. When my second also took his time, I kind of knew what I was doing. But this partially eroded my confidence, having two children who weren't strong early readers as I had been. (I had learned to read well before kindergarten, which made school itself a somewhat mystifying experience to me as a child. I couldn't grasp why the teacher talked so funny; I realize now that she must have been in the thrall of a scripted prereading curriculum.)

Despite my own concern about my boys' apparently late reading, we proceeded along happily until my oldest child reached the age to make his First Holy Communion. He couldn't read yet, and the dear lady who was the CCD teacher, and a retired elementary school teacher, was so concerned that I got concerned too. This was in spite of my having read several books such as *The Hurried*

Child by David Elkind, and *Better Late Than Early*, *Home-Grown Kids*, and others by Raymond and Dorothy Moore, all of which encouraged parents to let their children develop at their own pace.

Taken alone, this anxiety about reading may not have ended our unschooling adventure, but I had a deeper fear. Although I had been subscribing to *Growing Without Schooling* for several years and loved the publication, I worried that what we were doing wasn't very Catholic. None of the contributors to the magazine was Catholic, as far as I could tell. It really troubled me that not one of them ever spoke of faith, of God, of going to Mass or church.

I am uncomfortable in the role of pioneer, yet I was an unwitting pioneer of sorts. I was Catholic and I was definitely unschooling. Catholic homeschooling of any kind was still in its infancy, and while I gradually met other Catholic families who homeschooled, unschooling Catholics were simply unheard of. I didn't know where to begin to learn what I'd need to bolster my fledgling commitment to unschooling, and Catholic unschooling at that. Further, I felt that I lacked the know-how to research and analyze Church teaching about educational methods and philosophies. Even had I known where to begin in that project, I lacked the energy to pursue it, as by then I had a newborn, two-year-old, five-year-old, and seven-year-old. My husband was also becoming uncomfortable with unschooling. Consequently, when my oldest was in second grade, I chickened out and we left the world of unschooling.

Around this time, the National Association of Catholic Home Educators held its annual conference in Denver. Many wonderful speakers came, including one of the founders of Bethlehem Books, who leaned toward an unschooling style. Laura Berquist spoke about classical education. Joe Nowak, a computer engineer, spoke about computer technology in the homeschool (he was against it).

I loved it all, wanted it all. I wanted my children to learn Latin; be computer literate; be outdoor lovers; read great books; be curious about the world surrounding us; be athletes, musicians, artists, writers, and debaters; know how to take care of a house, car, family, and cook too!

Suddenly the solution to my dilemma was before my eyes, and it involved curriculum, schedules, and tests. I started cobbling together various school materials; I eagerly read every book which addressed Catholic homeschooling (few and far between in those years), and tended to change my method with every book and article I absorbed. I tried out Montessori, Charlotte Mason, classical . . .

Ultimately, this era became our long sidetrip into classical education. After a few years of my own research and experimenting, I entered in with my two oldest for about four years of heavy involvement. There were telephone and email tutoring sessions for them, and a consultant just for me. This consultant helped me lay out my school curriculum for my five children, who were then in first through ninth grades. While I appreciated the breadth of our plans, the reality in my home was a worried mother scurrying from child to child, room to room, frantically asking, "Have you done this?" and "Have you finished that?"

My oldest, in a vain effort to be free of a heavy workload not of his choosing, applied himself less and less to it. For his last two years of high school, he did little without being endlessly reminded. My next son, two years younger, had an easier time of writing, the subject which had so sorely tried his elder brother. This second son was also deeply and irrevocably drawn to computer games, beginning with Nintendo at age two (even though at the time we didn't have a computer or game system in the house). At the age of five, he would write out and solve lengthy addition problems for the sheer joy of it. But despite these encouraging beginnings, after eleven years of plowing though textbook math, he was completely fed up with it and stated flatly that he hated math. How could I have prevented this, committed as I now was to a structured classical curriculum?

Our third child showed her gifts in the arts. Math, the one thing that didn't come easily to her, became the prime indicator of how the day was going. As it seldom went well, the cloud would settle. A sense of failure led into a clinical depression which overtook our beloved daughter during her early teen years.

Although I was enduring doubts on a daily, even hourly basis, my two eldest progressed through and graduated from our Catholic classical homeschool. I saw that in the dreary, day-to-day, mind-numbing routine of trying to get their work done for me and for their tutors, they had lost all sense of wonder and delight. There had been no end to the work of school, and almost no satisfaction in learning any of it. At least that is how it appeared to me. Despite friends whose children thrived on the classical method, I had to admit that mine didn't.

Considerations like these were extremely hard for me to examine. I, too, felt like a failure. And to admit aloud that I was not doing it right generally invited well-meant remarks from my husband that they'd be better off in public school. The worry we felt was intense! But what to do? Unschooling, which had been so much fun, was godless as far as I knew. How could I revisit it? To go in such an unconventional direction seemed dicey. Nobody but aging flower children did school that way, as far as I could tell. And in Catholic homeschooling circles, I knew no aging flower children.

When my consultant from the classical program, who was worried about me as month after month I'd tell her I wasn't keeping up, gently suggested I try unschooling, it was beginning to look like a possibility. And then, late in the fall of 2004, a friend handed me a book she'd recently bought. It was Suzie's book: *Homeschooling with Gentleness, A Catholic Discovers Unschooling*. I devoured it. This book gave me the confidence to try unschooling again. Someone had thought it through and reached a well-reasoned conclusion: one could be a good Catholic and unschool too.

I jumped into the deep end of the unschool pool and it was refreshing. My then junior in high school decided not to try anything which sounded so risky and simply continued with his tutors and classical curriculum. My ninth grader, on the other hand, was almost beside herself with joy. In spite of her efforts, math had become so trying that she'd fallen further and further behind; she was working at a fifth-grade level. Returning to unschooling, my first big announcement to her was along the lines of, "How would you like to stop doing math?"

Months later I read of that announcement: "This is the happiest day of my life."

I had to wonder: Does school—regular school and even school-at-home school—really ruin children's lives? It might. Maybe it had been ruining mine. All I know is that freed from required reading, writing, and math, within six months my daughter felt vigorous enough to tackle book after book of math theory, physics, and astronomy. These were not textbooks, but scientific books written for the layman. She memorized vast swathes of Tolkien's and others' poetry, and prose from Booth Tarkington's *Penrod* books. She wrote stories and poetry, studied nature in the field and in numerous books of botany, pursued animal studies and the like, created art, played piano, took up the penny whistle and Indian flute, and learned figure skating and tap dancing. She taught herself Russian, then took months of classes with a native Russian speaker in an adult-education class. She has learned various organizing techniques along the way, as well as many other useful life and home-management skills. In her junior year she found a job in a greenhouse, and through her work there has since learned many of the native plants used in the landscaping business in Colorado.

I can hardly imagine a more successful unschooler than this daughter, absorbed as she has been in pursuing knowledge for its own sake. She is also a Catholic who has faced struggles in her faith, and yet continues in her faith. She will, perhaps, go to college in six months or a year, but only after traveling to the Russian Far East with a mission team this summer, and thus beginning to satisfy her desire to travel.

I have three younger children, currently ages fifteen, thirteen, and eleven. My fifteen-year-old's main interest is theater. He has acted in three different groups, sometimes concurrently, over the last four years, and participated in various acting workshops, as well as attending peer performances and professional productions. He started writing a lot, after I stopped requiring him to write anything. His most popular work, about a hapless knight named Bob, has completely cemented his reputation as an author. He goes to every movie and every youth group activity possible, and recently asked if he might attend the local part-time school, which caters to many homeschooling families we know.

Ironically, several of my friends have withdrawn their children from this same school, as it took away from the fun of homeschooling for them. One of them recently asked my input about unschooling; her children have some driving interests which she'd like them to have the time to pursue in depth. I find it strange to be asked about unschooling at the same time that my own unschooled children are asking to go to school! This fall the middle of my three younger children wants to attend high school, and as it seems a sensible sort of school, we're allowing him to go. He is taking child-led learning to a whole new level.

The youngest of the family is eleven and full of elevenings—like dancing to the loveliest of ballet music; making music of her own on three different instruments (four if you count singing); writing poems, stories, and letters to pen pals and relatives; raising chickens; doing a little baking; and being sweet to me and her dad. I'm not sure what would happen if I made her stop all that and learn her times tables and such. In response to anyone who might suggest that you don't have to stop any of it, just teach her those times tables for goodness sake, I would simply say: I don't know how to add in more. I am thrilled that she loves to write, and all the rest.

I do wonder if my earnest, well-meant, but very misguided correction of my older children's writing directly caused them to write less the older they got. I hesitate to tell the secret behind my four younger children writing so much, but here it is: I don't ask them to write any of it. And when they do write, I don't look at most of it. (I'm still too drawn to errors of spelling and so forth, and I don't want to ruin their writing by commenting unfavorably on it.)

Perhaps there are parents out there who are able to correct, endlessly, without it hurting. For my part, I've found that hurt feelings aren't to be shrugged off, although I tried to do just that for many years. I'm realizing more and more that our relationships with our children are extremely important. Being the one to correct their schoolwork put me in a position of too much power. I couldn't seem to learn the right way of correcting, still don't seem able to, and I'm thinking maybe I am just not supposed to. The serious approach didn't seem to work very well for some of my kids, so I'm trying the fun way now, which for me is definitely unschooling.

The children do their thing: karate, camping, music lessons, Russian, tap, ballet, theater, acting classes, drumming camp. We help get them places and pay for most of it. We're able to handle this financial aspect because we're not overwhelmed with private school tuition, but at times we take a step back and remind ourselves and them that this may not continue forever.

They pick up on a lot of basic life skills helping their dad with house and car upkeep. Quite a few political discussions go on. The kids cook, take care of things, have various jobs to earn money, some of which helps in a small way to pay for their classes or music supplies. Sometimes we'll borrow a movie based on our own interest in a documentary about General Custer or a slew of Ernst

Lubitsch movies from the 1930s and '40s, and whoever is around will watch and talk about it. Or I'll gather the kids together for a bit of reading aloud, or a catechism discussion.

We eat dinner together four or five times a week, and we pray the rosary in the evening, with whomever is home. As my husband works five nights a week, and one son works two nights a week, we have only one night when we're all home. This is our new normal: after twenty years of dinner together seven nights a week, we now have dinner together one or two nights a week.

Despite the usual tensions common to families, we recently had a successful family vacation which involved camping in tents for six nights in South Dakota, with five children aged eleven to twenty years. We pretty much had a blast, even counting the severe lightning and thunderstorms which greeted us almost every night. We cooked, ate, played, and slept within a few feet of each other, and in truth, it was fun to be so close, and really not that hard. I think unschooling has helped us to truly enjoy being together.

As our current newly graduated daughter makes her way, her father can't help but be impressed with her certainty and resolution. Even if she lacks certain classes which her brothers got through (all that math, for example), she has more goals toward which she's willing to work. She has chosen certain difficult things to learn, learned them well, and loved the learning even when it was hard. She is excited about this coming year when she'll be taking a high-school level chemistry class and a layperson's medical school course offered by the local university. She's gearing up for taking the SAT or ACT.

Her two older brothers had far fewer choices in our high-school homeschool, and what was given them to learn was learned well enough to pass and get a credit, and then left behind. This discouraging assessment of what went on in our homeschool is fairly accurate, they'll tell you. But they're recovering from it, gradually.

Looking back upon the Catholic classical program we used, I think of the wonderful people I met, as well as my appreciation for the spectrum of subjects and the method itself, and I know why it was so hard for me to leave the program, to admit it wasn't working with my children. With the benefit of three years of renewed unschooling, I can see now that I've been too harsh in faulting myself. Not only were we right to return to unschooling, but the road back was instructive as well. And the road ahead—who knows where it will lead? At this juncture we are filled again with interests and aspirations. I hope, amid my ever present uncertainty, that many of our dreams and good desires will come to fruition.

An update on the Wagner kids: Amy reports that her eldest son is serving in the United States Coast Guard. Her second son, a history major and avid gamer, is in Army ROTC. Her twenty-year-old daughter is a sophomore at a Catholic college; she is loving the experience. The second youngest son, who was so into theater, is in an Emergency Medical Technician program. The youngest son is a junior in public high school, which is where he really wanted to be. Her youngest, now thirteen, is continuing in learning various forms of dance. Amy's "ever present uncertainty" (and general anxiety) have considerably lessened as the children grow up and make their way.

CHAPTER FIVE

Leonie's Family: Let the Mother Go Out to Play

Leonie Westenberg and her husband are the parents of seven sons who are aged thirteen to twenty-eight. Their family lives in Australia, where they have been homeschooling for the past twenty-three years. Leonie is a Kumon Education Supervisor, and she writes a blog about her family life which can be found at http://livingwithoutschool.blogspot.com/; she also maintains the blog on Catholic unschooling at http://unschoolingcatholics.blogspot.com/.

> *If mothers could learn to do for themselves what they do for their children . . . we should have happier households. Let the mother go out to play! If she would have the courage to let everything go when life becomes too tense, and just take a day, or half a day, out in the fields, or with a favourite book, or in a picture gallery looking long and well at just two or three pictures, or in bed, without the children, life would go on far more happily for both children and parents.*
>
> —Charlotte Mason, *School Education*

This quotation describes our Catholic unschooling: playing, experiencing life with joy, exploring passions within the rich, sacramental life of the Catholic Church. This is why we are Catholics who unschool, who live and learn.

Picture this: It is 9:00 A.M. on a Monday morning. My youngest son Anthony, aged twelve, is lying on the family room sofa, reading. Another son Thomas, aged fifteen, is playing Mario Cart on the Wii game playing system. I chat to them about the saint for today, St. Ephrem. I mention that St. Ephrem was the first to use the female voice in hymns. Alexander, aged sixteen, does a Google search on the life and times of St. Ephrem.

Then I start my home business work, asking these younger three sons what their plans are for the day. What time do part time jobs start? When are they planning to do Kumon Math? Does Alexander have an assignment to work on for Italian, a subject he is studying through the university? They assure me of their plans. But their first priority of the day is this new game on the video game system.

I am happy; they are happy. The schoolwork, the learning, is not separated from life but is woven amongst our many interests and activities. We don't see learning and the rest of life as separate pursuits. My sons' days are not very school-ish and are mostly managed by themselves—we just talk the night before or in the morning about the day-to-day, and every few months or so about what is happening in the bigger picture. We talk about anything that needs doing, enthusiasms and goals and have-tos, problems, issues, concerns. This becomes an education for autodidacts.

Our family strives to live in an atmosphere of learning, yet we still do bits and pieces of more formal work. We read and learn and talk all the time, and we supplement this with our extra curricular activities: serving at Mass, piano lessons, outings, activities with other homeschoolers, and volunteer work in our parish. But any formal work gets squeezed into life, not the other way around. The formal work doesn't run our life, but is just a thing to push in here and shove in there; it's like housework really! Everything gets done, just at odd moments and odd times. I may mop the floor late at night before bed, and the kids may do some math and religion in the car on the way to ice skating.

This is our form of Catholic unschooling; it is not defined by what we don't do, but by what we do. Someone once said to me that he thought my kids were clever and intelligent, but he couldn't figure out how since we did so little schoolwork. He was probably thinking of all we do not do, rather than of all that we do. Unschooling isn't about not doing schoolwork; it is about play and learning; it is about life. It is about doing. We spend time with our children, and we respect them as individuals. We follow their interests; we follow our own. We explore and learn with each other. Ours is not necessarily the didactic model of teaching but the collegial one of sharing and learning together. As Pope Benedict XVI has said in his *Letter to Romans on Education*:

> The educative relationship is, however, above all the meeting of two freedoms, and successful education is the formation of the right use of freedom. Little by little the child grows, he becomes an adolescent and then a youth; we must therefore accept the risk of freedom, always remaining attentive to help him correct mistaken ideas and choices. That which we must never do is to go along with him in his errors, pretend not to see them, or worse, to share in them, as if they were the new frontiers of human progress. Education cannot, therefore, do without that authoritativeness that makes the exercise of authority credible . . . it is acquired above all by consistency in one's own life and by personal involvement, an expression of true love. The educator is thus a witness of truth and of goodness. (Angelus Message, February 6, 2008)

While educating our children, while living and learning as a family, we educate and form ourselves: our characters, our souls.

For us, this mutual growth is the Catholic influence in unschooling. As Catholic unschoolers, do we force our Faith and practices onto the children? I doubt it, because as unschoolers, we use a less didactic model of education; unschooling trusts the learner to be in charge of his or her own learning. We try to inspire, to be role models.

We aim to create a family culture of Catholic practices, so that living the liturgical year is like breathing. It is part of what we do and part of who we are. I think that it is just as important that we parent well, giving the boys a good childhood and passing on the Faith, as that we provide a good education. The boys can catch up on the academics later, if necessary, although we do see them learning all the time. It is harder, though, to work through problems in parenting and relationships, so I am aiming for joy in our life together, and trusting that the rest will follow. And so far, it has.

The Catholic Encyclopedia says of St. John Bosco, one of our mentors in Catholic unschooling:

> In his rules he wrote: "Frequent Confession, frequent Communion, daily Mass: these are the pillars which should sustain the whole edifice of education." . . . He thoroughly believed in play as a means of arousing childish curiosity—more than this, he places it among his first recommendations, and for the rest he adopted St. Philip Neri's words: "Do as you wish, I do not care so long as you do not sin." (Saxton, "St. Giovanni Melchior Bosco")

Do as you wish, as long as you do not sin. I find here confirmation that Catholics can choose to unschool, without fear of compromising their Faith. The Faith can be lived and shared in the same way that a family shares in each individual's educational life: their thoughts, their interests, their activities. Education in life and the Faith happens, sometimes through osmosis, and sometimes through a more rigorous study.

In his homily one Sunday, our parish priest mentioned that our faith should grow; it should not simply remain the faith we had at age twelve. It should be a living faith. I find the same is true of our learning, our homeschooling. It is not static, resting contentedly under a label, but it is an organic education that changes as the children and family change. We learn and grow in our faith, in our knowledge, and in who and what we are.

Let the mother, and the father, and the children go out to play. The emphasis on play is what first drew both my husband and me to unschooling. As teachers ourselves, we knew the importance of play. As parents, we had seen our toddlers and preschoolers learning while playing. Unschooling seemed a natural progression to us.

We now have seven sons, aged thirteen to twenty-eight; my husband is in the military and we have moved many, many times during our unschooling life. But when I was first introduced to the concept of homeschooling I had three young boys, the oldest aged five, and we were living in a small city in New South Wales, Australia. Through the local parish, I met a mother of seven girls, all of whom were homeschooled. I was working part time and my first thought was, "What about socialization—for the mother?" Yet I realized that this mother continued her career as a part-time music teacher while homeschooling her lively, friendly, curious girls. The seed of homeschooling was planted in my mind.

I went to a bookshop and ordered a book on homeschooling: *Teach Your Own* by John Holt. It was here that I encountered the term "unschooling." Holt had vignettes in the book describing families and their ways of unschooling, of following children's interests, of living and learning together without formal schooling. I found myself mentally nodding and agreeing my way through the book, and I couldn't stop reading whole sections out loud to my husband.

It wasn't long before we were both sold on the idea of passions, of crazes, of play, learning all the while. Our oldest son was already reading; he kept a journal and scrapbook, and he was madly interested in war history and in numbers. We could see how just following his lead in a busy, stimulating, homey environment could foster learning. And so unschooling is how we started homeschooling.

Every now and then over the years, though, as we moved and had more children and miscarriages and health problems, I would read something else about homeschooling. I would think, *Maybe we should incorporate more ideas from Charlotte Mason . . . more classical education . . . the tools of learning . . . more religion.* I wasn't Catholic at this stage, but my husband was, and we were raising our children in the Faith. I'd try a schedule, a few textbooks, and a unit study. Eventually I would set these aside and we'd be back to unschooling. It just seemed to fit our very busy lifestyle, complementing our involvement in church, homeschool groups, and the community; our paid work; our outside activities and hobbies; our home renovations as we moved yet again; and our constant stream of visitors. Add in all the reading and movies and music we loved . . . Who had time for school?

In my doubt-filled moments, I'd read more about unschoolers and feel reassured. Then when I became a Catholic in January 1995, my reading of Church history and of the lives of the saints provided additional support for my unschooling. Our life of learning seemed most respectful of the parent-child relationship. Moreover, it mirrored the relationship of Christ and His Church and allowed for the exercise of free will.

My husband, as I mentioned, has been supportive of my role as an unschooling, homeschooling mother from the outset. He too believes intrinsically in the concept of learning all the time, and he has always trusted me to know our sons. Given his full-time work and study, I have been the one to spend more time with the boys, and he appreciates just how well I know them. His main areas of homeschooling interaction with our sons have been math and providing some sense of discipline.

It was the Internet that eventually introduced me to the idea of radical unschooling, that is, unschooling in everything, in all of life, not just education. Radical unschooling was very liberating for me. I could feel myself throwing away checklists, embracing thinking outside the box, becoming free to be me. Or so I thought. After a while, I found that I tended to hold myself accountable to some idealistic picture of the perfect unschool. I'd ask myself, *Isn't this coercion? Shouldn't I let the kids make all their own choices?* Overthinking every little thing soon became wearying. Just as I had let go of more formal homeschooling, so I had to let go of this concept of pure unschooling and of my monolithic vision of the perfect unschooling mother. I decided, instead, to discard labels, to live with joy and to embrace what felt most comfortable for us and for our Faith.

We now have the further advantage and reassurance of having seen our own unschooled, homeschooled graduates. They have done well at university and at jobs, they are good people, and they practice their Faith. On top of all that, they still have room for growing and learning, as do my husband and I.

As we continue to live and learn together, we can relax and enjoy what we have discovered, namely, our unschooling style, which is learning and playing in an atmosphere of respect. Unschooling is family-centered learning through passions and play and faith, and for us this is a good fit.

CHAPTER SIX

Terri's Family: Do I Have Time for Unschooling?

Terri Aquilina and her husband Mike have six children aged seven to twenty-one years old. Their family lives in Pennsylvania where they have been homeschooling for the last fifteen years. Terri's writing has appeared in New Covenant *magazine,* Family Foundations, *and* The Pittsburgh Catholic. *With her husband, Mike, she co-authored the essay "Milk and Mystery: On Breastfeeding and the Theology of the Body," which appeared in* Catholic for a Reason, Volume IV: Scripture and the Mystery of Marriage and Family Life *(Emmaus Road Press). Terri holds a bachelor's degree in Individual and Family Studies from Penn State University. Raised a Lutheran, she has been a Roman Catholic since 1991.*

Education is not filling a bucket, but lighting a fire.

—W.B. Yeats

I have to start out with the confession that I never planned to homeschool, much less unschool. I was hoping to have a large family; I believed that I certainly wouldn't have time to teach my kids at home. When my first child, Michael, was about four, my husband brought up the idea of homeschooling, so I read a book about it. I found that I had been right—it would be much too time consuming.

As Michael got closer to kindergarten age, though, it seemed less and less like a good idea to send him to school. He would be turning five in August and would be eligible for all-day kindergarten in September. He was very bright and learning how to read on his own. But how could I send him away all day? He was a little pipsqueak of a kid and definitely not a morning person. He would have been that kid on the bus with uncombed hair, wrinkled clothes, and no breakfast. I decided I could surely do kindergarten at home. How hard could kindergarten be?

So off we started on our homeschooling adventure. Being the daughter of a teacher and of an elementary school principal, I was sure I knew exactly what to do. If I couldn't have a real classroom, at least we could buy an official curriculum and provide plenty of other books and worksheets and puzzles. So I purchased a kindergarten curriculum, and for a while it went smoothly. Michael had never done workbooks before, and he thought they were fun. For a week or two. Then he started to question my assignments. "Why can't I do the last page first?" and "Why do I have to put the sticker of Cookie Monster's head on the place where the dotted lines are?" My obsessive-compulsive teacher persona panicked. Of course you start at the front of the workbook and continue through to the end without skipping pages, and every sticker goes in its place. He would ask me such questions over and over, until eventually it occurred to me that it really didn't matter. From then on he did whichever pages appealed to him and happily stuck Cookie Monster's head onto various Muppet bodies.

Again I felt we were succeeding, but as the years went by and his sisters started joining our homeschool, Michael became less and less willing to do his assignments. "But why do I have to do math?" and "Why do I have to learn this?" His questions made me think. I had been reading John Holt and learning about unschooling. I talked with my son about it, and we made a deal that if he did well on his standardized tests for fifth grade (mandated by the state of Pennsylvania), he could unschool. He did well on the tests and began unschooling. Fifth grade was the last year he did math until he decided on his own to do some, in eleventh grade, in preparation for the SAT.

What a blessing it was to quit our frequent arguing over whether or not he should have to learn this or that. We have always called him our junior lawyer, since he would invariably prefer to argue for hours about why he should have to do a math page rather than to take ten minutes and simply do the work. I have Michael to thank for our family's jump into unschooling.

There are many ideas about right and wrong ways to unschool, but I'm sure that what every family does is different. I like to sit down with each child at the beginning of the year to discuss what he or she is interested in learning, and what resources might be necessary. We do use some bits and pieces of curricula, but always of the children's choosing.

Two of my girls have used several years of Sonlight history because they enjoy historical fiction. I have a number of math textbooks and several years of *Maps, Charts, Graphs* workbooks. In Pennsylvania we have to turn in a portfolio with student work samples at the end of the year. I do require a page of math (without doodles) every once in a while in order to have something to put into their folder. The kids usually do enough writing and art on their own so that there are a few things for me to choose from when we are due to report. Over the years I have noticed that we are getting away from the workbook pages and moving into a more narrative style of portfolio. For example, we might list "managed own allowance money and budgeted savings for special events, shopping, gift buying, and vacations" for the math section.

It has been great to see how the kids learn so much about the things they are interested in. They have not learned a lot of formal math! Michael, now nineteen, still doesn't have the times tables memorized, but he is holding down a full-time job as a software programmer for a financial institution, and he regularly uses formulas for computing interest in his programs. He has been able to pick up any math he needs because he now sees a purpose for it.

But how has unschooling (versus traditional homeschooling) made a difference for my children? First and foremost, by allowing the children to attend Mass every day if they so choose. Since my primary concern for them is that they will grow up to be good churchgoing Catholics, unschooling has helped them take a huge step toward that goal.

Unschooling also gives the whole family time to volunteer. For me, a big part of being a Catholic is helping others, and I hope my kids grow up to think so too. Our children have volunteered for parish activities, helped with babysitting at diocesan NFP programs, and entertained the little ones at La Leche League events. One of my daughters volunteers with me at our library bookstore. They all realize that their parents consider serving others to be important.

Another benefit of our unschooling, and one that will help to produce good Catholics, is that our kids have the time to sit around and talk. They are able to ask us questions, and they can listen in as we discuss events of the day or what the Pope said when he visited the United States. We don't have to make special times to talk about religion; it comes up naturally. We are able to share in what the kids are thinking or worrying about. We are available if they have questions about the Faith or regarding what they have heard people say about Catholics.

I would like our children someday to be sensible Catholic adults who know how to think for themselves—adults who can find out what they need to know. Because we have the time, we are able to discuss our interests. The kids often report back on what they have found out about how a new movie differs from the book, or what a presidential candidate thinks on certain issues. My kids know how to shop for good deals and how to save money. They are not embarrassed to ask questions.

I also want my children to be able to follow up on their interests. With a family of eight, that means lots of different pursuits. Our mealtimes usually involve loud discussions about such things as whether *The Phantom of the Opera* is a classic novel (I say it isn't), and whether it matters (it doesn't). We have talked about modesty, municipal bonds, whether the Colin Firth Darcy is better than the Matthew Macfadyen Darcy, or whether the frog Webkinz is cuter than the panda. There is plenty of time to talk and everybody gets a chance to join in the discussion.

My husband works at home so the whole family is able to spend quite a portion of our days with one another. We don't have to go on expensive vacations to get our together time. We are more likely to hop in the van and go for ice cream and a visit to a used bookstore. The children are able to see their dad at work; they know they have to be quiet if he is doing a radio show or taking a business call. The older kids have gone with him to talks he gives, and they help to sell books. They don't think of the work adults do as something mysterious and scary, and they are at ease in social situations because we have never excluded them.

We have the time to learn to be kind. I am hoping for kind adults, and unschooling allows me the time to repeat for the millionth time that day, "If you would like to use the toy, please ask nicely, and she will give it to you when she is finished." It is somewhat easy to be kind to friends, but harder with siblings. My older kids help the younger ones and are terrific at entertaining them. The younger ones give the older ones the unconditional love that teenagers really seem to need.

I've been saying it all along: the great thing about unschooling is that it gives us time. My kids have time to be kids. They play outside for hours, making up elaborate games with Polly Pocket dolls or Barbies. They help our elderly neighbors plant flowers and garden. The older kids have time to be with their friends. They can help me by cooking or babysitting. When Michael worked at our local library, he was available to work any time of day. One of my daughters works as a mother's helper and because we unschool, she can work during the daytime when many mothers are anxious for a little help. She is going to be a wonderful mom herself someday with all this practice.

Unschooling gives my kids time to do ordinary things. And some extraordinary things. My oldest two daughters were in a Girl Scout troop for homeschoolers; they loved it and were sad when the troop folded. They complained to me that they would never get to see their friends. I didn't have the time or energy to start a club for them, and so I suggested they start their own club, with the proviso that I was not going to plan it or be in charge of it.

Mary Agnes and Rosemary gladly took up the challenge. They chose friends to invite, decided on a day and time, and planned meetings and dues. Their club has been going strong for four years now. They have done crafts, played board games, showed off their stamps, rocks and coin collections, and taken hikes. They have worked as mother's helpers to raise money to feed the hungry. They have taken cookies to nursing-home residents. Mary Agnes was even invited to speak at a diocesan education conference about starting a girls' club; the talk was so popular at preregistration that the diocese asked her to give it twice.

The best part of the club, though, is the friendships that have developed and deepened. Running their club has taught my daughters to appreciate others' feelings and to be patient with those younger than themselves. They have also learned the advantages of planning ahead, since Mom is never happy to have to run to the craft store at 8:30 P.M. for Mod Podge.

Along with girls' club, my daughter Gracie's big interest is ballet. She has been taking classes for four years now, and as with so many of our activities, I am not sure we would have the time if we had a lot of schoolwork to do. Ballet has helped her develop physical strength, broaden her cultural horizons, and has been good for her self-esteem as well. In a family with five girls, it can be nice to have something that is yours, something no one else does but you.

Beyond giving my children the time to pursue what interests them, unschooling has allowed them the freedom to read. Some people say that unless kids are *forced* to read great literature, they will never consider it. Our Rosemary showed us that this is not true. As soon as she could read, she gravitated toward the classics. She was very young when she got hooked on C.S. Lewis. My husband thought she might like the medieval romances that inspired Lewis, so he introduced her to Walter Map's Arthurian epic, *The Quest of the Holy Grail.* Rosemary couldn't get enough. From there, he introduced her to Cervantes' hilarious parody of the knightly romances, *Don Quixote*, which they read together (with Mike censoring on the fly as he read aloud). Rosemary is a teen now and still reading the good old stuff: Jane Austen, the Bronte sisters, and J. R. R. Tolkien, in addition to more recent literature like Regina Doman's fairy tale novels.

My eldest, Michael, found the time for a great adventure. It began when his grandmother was crippled by a stroke. Since Michael was not bound by a curriculum, he was able to travel to help his aunts and uncles care for her. He was eager to work, but he got bored pretty quickly when there wasn't much for him to do. My husband Mike suggested that Michael use his downtime to write a book about St. Jude, a project Michael was always trying to convince someone else to tackle.

Mike suggested a number of ancient and modern resources that could be found online, and Michael was off and running. He wrote most of the book while he was at his grandmother's house, but his education didn't end with the writing. It turns out that publishers are not out there just waiting to print every teenager's first book!

Michael sent out his manuscript, and it got rejected. He sent it out again. And again. At long last, the Daughters of St. Paul decided to publish it, but then came more work. Their academic reviewers raised some historical and theological questions and requested some changes, which meant that Michael had to go back to his research. This phase may have been harder for him than the actual writing. Finally the book was published with beautiful illustrations. Michael is quite proud of the book but decided that writing books is way too much trouble for way too little money. Still, I was delighted to hand in his page proofs for his school district portfolio that year.

Another unschooling adventure for our family was a trip to Rome. A Capuchin priest friend of ours, Father Ronald Lawler, was planning a business trip to Italy, and we jokingly asked if he would take our kids with him. Before we knew it, we were *all* planning a trip. As unschoolers, we didn't have to get scheduled schoolwork done before we could go. Nor did we have work piled up after we came home. We used our time to learn some Italian and pored over books on Roman history and sights. We even watched movies that had been filmed in Rome—our favorite was *Roman Holiday*. Father Ronald helped us prepare by telling us stories about his many trips to the Eternal City. He taught all the kids to pronounce *gelato*.

After we arrived in Rome, Father Ronald arranged for us to attend a papal audience and personally meet Pope John Paul II. We treasure our photos with him. My husband and son were also able to attend a Mass in the papal apartment, although Michael spent the whole time with his feet crammed under a kneeler—it seems he had dressed in such a hurry that he put on sneakers instead of dress shoes! The whole week was a delight. Father Ronald died a year and a half after our trip. We still miss him terribly, but we are all glad we had the freedom to drop everything and spend so much time with him in Rome.

Unschooling has been beneficial to my children, but it has also been a big help to me. I have seen how much my children learn when they are left to choose what to learn about. They impress me with their zeal for knowledge and their self-confidence, and I know that they are indeed learning, which is gratifying for a mom. Since I am not spending hours a day officially teaching them, I am able to use my time to counsel moms about breastfeeding, volunteer on our diocesan NFP Advisory Board, and serve on the board of our local library. The kids help with these things and, truly, it is all a learning experience. When it comes right down to it, the only schooling my family has time for is unschooling.

BETTY
St. POVER

CHAPTER SEVEN

Maria's Family: Living on Adrenaline and Grace

Maria Peceli and her husband Steve are the parents of four spirited children who are aged ten to thirteen. Their family lives in California, where they have been homeschooling since their oldest was ready for kindergarten. Maria, a former schoolteacher, operates with her daughters a jewelry business from home, writes the blog Living on Adrenaline and Grace (http://tater-tots-and-ladybug-love.blogspot.com) *and is currently working as a publicist for Father John Waiss, helping him to promote his latest book,* Born to Love.

> *God's love can only unleash its power when it is allowed to change us from within. We have to let it break through the hard crust of our indifference, our spiritual weariness, our blind conformity to the spirit of this age. Only then can we let it ignite our imagination and shape our deepest desires.*
>
> —Pope Benedict XVI, Address to Youth, World Youth Day XXIII

Many people have a difficult time grasping the concept of unschooling, precisely because of what it isn't. You might say that it isn't the norm as we know it; perhaps the term itself sounds negative, implying folks are just being lazy, doing nothing. Or it sounds like a protest. But even if we start with unschooling as merely the negation of schooling, we might want to ask ourselves the question, Why is that so unappealing? When I consider my own fairly typical education, wanting something else doesn't seem like a bad thing.

Before becoming a teacher, before becoming a mom, and before becoming an unschooler, I was a student. As a student I learned to perform, rather than be concerned with knowledge or virtue. I could conform, mimic, imitate, and do what I was told, but I wasn't inspired. From these early experiences I grew dependent on the feedback of teachers and others, overly attached to their response to my performance. Sadly, I still desire to be affirmed. I still experience the effects of that system, and often I still want the reassurance and reward of a gold star next to my name. When I became a parent, I asked myself, *Is that what I want for my children?*

And yet, I didn't exactly choose unschooling, it sort of chose me. For us, unschooling happened by necessity. You see, even though the word *unschooler* has been known to conjure up images of abandonment and neglect, our family came to discover unschooling precisely in order to avoid those evils. The freedom to use whatever method inspired my children, be it Charlotte Mason's or Maria Montessori's or the child's own ideas, had to take precedence over what I wanted. Instead of imposing my carefully thought-out methodology, I felt that it was my job to provide a smorgasbord of topics to stimulate their hunger for knowledge. And unschooling gave me that permission, as it were.

My children were born close together: my oldest was only three years old when my fourth was born. So when this oldest was five, and by society's standards ready to jump into that ocean which is kindergarten, I still had two children in diapers and four children who woke at night with varied regularity.

Because I didn't want to abandon the children due to my exhaustion, and because I did not desire to neglect their interests, I simply let a few things go. Laundry was in, formal table work was out. Eating was in, mandated reading was out.

Now don't laugh. I remember when I was starting out homeschooling. I may—just possibly—have had preconceived notions about how things were going to be. But then God threw at me something called life, and thanks to job layoffs, financial stress, sleeplessness, and other circumstances, I learned to let go and live with those constant companions, trusting that my children would learn and want to learn.

And that is why instead of doing seat work, we jaunted off to the library and concerts and museums. We learned through experiences. I listened to the chatter of my little ones' innocent voices going on about their interests, and we checked out books on those subjects.

For our oldest daughter, believe it or not, we studied the Impressionists during our year of kindergarten and bought two sets of art postcards from Dover. We played Go, Paint!—our version of Go, Fish!—and all of the children became familiar with the names Gauguin, Cezanne, Monet, Degas, Renoir, Cassatt, and Van Gogh. From there we went on to read lots of Mike Venezia books. The children's knowledge of art history broadened so that when Degas' *Little Dancer* came through our neck of the woods, we went to see her and they knew who she was. That was six years ago, and the knowledge has stuck with them. Recently, on a trip to a local art museum, my oldest daughter was able to share the story of Romulus and Remus when she saw a mosaic table piece. Needless to say, I was thrilled.

To spark a love of geography when the kids were young, we hosted an international postcard exchange. Through various sources that I knew from the Internet, to friends and family traveling, I took advantage of my shy nature (ahem) and asked people to send us postcards from their travels. Posting a map of the world on the kitchen wall, we logged many postcards from such exotic locations as Tasmania and Australia, as well as local places like Mount Shasta, CA and Twain Harte, CA. Considering I was born in Venezuela and my husband's family is from Croatia, we were able to acquire postcards from those regions. We saw how effective a method of learning unschooling could be when we took advantage of what was at hand and capitalized on it.

Reading good literature as well as articles about current events has laid a strong foundation for my children's learning, and for their lives. Along with living our Faith, our reading and the ensuing conversations have been the cement which bonds us together. As a mom who reads aloud to her kids, I have learned how invaluable discussion is. Until I had experienced it myself, no one could have convinced me of the richness and depth of learning that occurs in this way.

When I set aside my plans and just spent time with my children—baking and playing games, reading and discussing life—we found freedom to explore, which opened up a world of wonder. Through our curious exploration, I found both that my children learned and that they loved learning. For me this was a real discovery.

I realize now something else as well. Through unschooling, God has granted me what I most deeply desired. He has given me children who thrive in an intimate relationship with us, their parents. I have struggled with intimacy in the past, and had moments of trying to avoid it, but God knew the way to gently reach my heart. Unschooling brought about intimacy in our family by allowing us to open up with each other—and to be ourselves.

This new intimacy also brought about a major development in my spiritual life: I finally figured out that I don't have to perform. Like a considerate parent, God places before us exactly what we need, and then lets us think we discovered it. Isn't it just like Him to unschool us in a deeply personal relationship?

As my children grow, I notice in them certain desires for greater structure, and we continue to experiment with how to fulfill these needs. For one of my children the answer was Saxon Math, for another we used phonics cards because he liked them. Increasingly they hear their dad and me talking about things we believe are important in their education, and why they are important. I find it exciting to see that what works for one child may not work for another, and I am convinced that the uniqueness of each individual brings a richness to the whole family.

With this addition of more structure, would I still call what we do unschooling? Yes, because our home is still an intimate, loving learning environment in which we discuss what is important and why it is important, with the people on earth who are most important to us. And this learning together, day in and day out, continues to teach me that my relationship with my children is more important than my curriculum choices for them.

In my home we struggle financially, and I sometimes get outside pressure to put the kids in school and go to work, as if my working will solve all of the problems. It seems obvious to me, however, that by going to work and sending the children out of the home I would just be substituting a new set of problems for my old familiar ones. I find it especially troubling that because I used to be a professional teacher, people think that somehow my work homeschooling doesn't measure up. My view is quite the opposite. As Chesterton wrote in his essay "The Emancipation of Domesticity,"

> How can it be a large career to tell other people's children about the rule of Three and a small career to tell one's own children about the universe? How can it be broad to be the same thing to everyone, and narrow to be everything to

> someone? No; a woman's function is laborious, but because it is gigantic, not because it is minute. (46)

Homeschooling has been a marvelous journey of studying my children and how they think, and also of learning to let go of my preconceived notions. I certainly don't have all the answers, and the experience is very learn-as-you-go, but I am thoroughly enjoying watching my children develop into the people that God made them to be. I'm not sure that I would have believed that unschooling could work; fortunately life nudged me into it. Maybe that's why they say "It's good to give thanks in all things," for you never know where the adventure will take you.

CHAPTER EIGHT

Beate's Family: The Reluctant Unschoolers

Beate and her husband are the parents of five children aged five to fifteen. Their family lives in Texas, down the street from Beate's sister Sabine. Beate studied education and childhood development in college, and worked in a kindergarten before her first child was born; she went from being a teacher to a homeschooling mom. Beate and her sister sporadically maintain the blog Catholic Mommas.

> *If we have no silence, God is not heard in our music. If we have no rest, God does not bless our work. If we twist our lives out of shape in order to fill every corner of them with action and experience, God will silently withdraw from our hearts and leave us empty.*
>
> —Thomas Merton
> *No Man Is an Island*

Unschooling. What is it? I'm not sure I can give you a positive definition, but I can definitely tell you what it isn't. It is neither unparenting, nor is it being undisciplined, uninvolved, unmotivated, or unmindful. It might be somewhat scheduled, and it can involve taking classes. It manifests itself as a unique composite in every home, yet at the very least, unschoolers are interesting and interested.

Much validation for unschooling can be found in various objections to it. "My child would never learn math" is a comment I've heard more than once. I want to ask, "Don't you cook? play games? budget? figure your gas mileage? tell time? Do your kids have a bank account? Can they figure out their interest?" Math is all around us—it's just that some children have a greater affinity for it than others. These are the ones who will be more likely to go on in their mathematical endeavors.

Another frequent worry is that the children will just vegetate in front of the television all day. I've found that my children would much rather be busy doing things, especially with me, than just sitting around. Of course that means that I need to be actively engaged in their lives, mindful of their interests, passions, and pursuits.

Our family's journey to unschooling has been one of barely discernable baby steps. It is only in looking back now that I can clearly see the path from the very beginning. Even in the mid to late 1980s, while studying educational theory in college, I was drawn to educational reform. People like Maria Montessori, Rudolf Steiner, David Elkind, Constance Kamii, and Mary Baratta-Lorton planted seeds in my mind, seeds that would grow, ideas that would change throughout the next decade. Whatever their differences, these educators all agreed that every child has the ability to learn. I reiterated this philosophy to the principal who interviewed me for my first teaching job, and then I told myself that the somewhat condescending smile on her face must have been in my imagination.

At that time, we were given yearly goals to meet, but had the freedom to meet them on our own terms. I taught kindergarten, and on many days the children's collaborative building projects would take over a large portion of the room and remain there, much to the dismay of the janitor. I was naive enough to imagine that most schools operated with this type of freedom, or at least had the children's best interests in mind. Our vice principal had attended seminars about a circular lesson model based on Gardner's Multiple Intelligence theory, and we were moving away from grades toward portfolio assessment.

When our daughter was born in 1994, I quit teaching to stay home with her. At my midwife's office, I picked up a copy of *Mothering* magazine and became a subscriber; in its pages I first encountered the term *unschooling*. Preposterous! Why would anyone want her child to be uneducated? (Looking back, I realize that the Holy Spirit has a great sense of humor.) While I felt strongly about the importance of spending those first three years with my daughter, certainly at some point my daughter would attend school.

My oldest niece began kindergarten in the fall of 1995. When my sister became frustrated that her daughter's classroom environment was entirely unlike the classrooms in the school where I had taught, I encouraged her to trust that it would be better next year. I totally dismissed her idea of homeschooling. In college I had gained tremendous insight into child development and the way children learn, and it was simply inconceivable to me that homeschooling was a good idea. Surely, my niece's situation was an isolated incident, and the following year would bring a positive learning experience. By the time 1999 rolled around, two of my nieces had a combined experience of three different elementary schools and eight teachers; I knew beyond a doubt that I would not send any of my children to school, for the first few years at any rate.

Out came the ABCs, the calendar, and assorted bulletin board materials. Soon the second bedroom was transformed into a kindergarten classroom, and school at home began. Sarah and her cousin did the letter of the week and played math games throughout the spring and parts of the summer of 1999. In October, we moved into a new home, and my already fussy newborn rebelled at the total change of environment. School was on hold. Kindergarten wasn't required in our state at any rate, so we had another year of freedom. During that time I discovered the Internet and Charlotte Mason. Real books? Perfect, I love books!

Those were halcyon days of finger-painting, picture books, math manipulatives, and homemade play dough. I wrote down Sarah's narrations and she wrote pages and pages of her own stories. Still, letters and sounds made absolutely no sense to my otherwise bright five-year-old. I trusted that she would learn to read when she was ready, thinking it would be the next year. It wasn't. It didn't happen the next year either, or the year after.

It did happen eventually, but meanwhile, trusting in her God-given ability to learn was getting to be difficult. Although I encouraged other moms on homeschooling lists, I was secretly despairing inside. I did all the right things, so why couldn't she read? She loved books, loved being read to, and comprehended complicated stories. Was there something wrong? *Children learn at their own pace*, an inner voice said. *Trust some more*. "Put Me first," came a gentle voice as I gazed at the crucifix. Deep sigh. *Okay, Lord, I will trust*.

When we started the 2001 school year, I was determined that we would be more organized and stick to the well-crafted plan I had outlined. Trust was good, but clearly I needed to put in more effort. Yes, scope and sequence would be adhered to, albeit in a Charlotte Mason fashion.

Joyfully pregnant with our fourth child, I was sure the initial tiredness would soon be gone. But the first trimester sickness didn't go away, and the energy didn't come back. We trudged along until February 15, 2002. That was the day my sweet five-year-old was air-lifted to the hospital after falling off a picnic table. She had stopped breathing by the time the helicopter arrived and didn't regain consciousness for almost twelve hours. When she came to, "Mommy, I love you," became the most precious words I have ever heard. She healed rapidly, but was back in PICU three weeks later after contracting Steven's Johnson Syndrome as a result of the anti-seizure medicine she had been given. The trauma doctor and her neurologist gently told me that she might die. I knew she wouldn't, and I was right, but the recovery was painful. She came home three days before her sister was born. School was no longer a priority; being with my children was. Suddenly, the important stuff was more evident than ever before.

The following autumn, I evaluated where we were educationally and was surprised at how much the children had learned. Perhaps my role as teacher wasn't as important as I had initially thought. Maybe just being Mom was enough.

Still, I would never have considered myself an unschooler, so when a friend invited me to join an unschooling list, I was somewhat taken aback. *Why on earth does she think that I would be a good fit for an unschooling forum?* I wondered at the time. When she told me who some of the members were, I know my eyebrows disappeared into my hairline. *What?!* These were all moms I very much admired as parents and educators; mostly, though, I admired them for the relationships they had with their children. My friend assured me that as a relaxed Charlotte Mason type homeschooler, I would fit right in.

Join I did, and I was instantly embraced and soon challenged by this awesome group of women. Not surprisingly, it was the radical unschoolers who first shocked and then most inspired me. I spent the next several months pondering and reflecting on what the Holy Spirit was trying to tell me.

It was easy for me to discern that formal early childhood education was trying in vain to duplicate the home environment. Children were drawn to the kitchen center because helping Mom at home in a real kitchen wasn't "educational" enough for the experts. Colors and shapes were taught in stilted silly ways because they weren't being learned in the course of day-to-day activities and conversations at home. I saw clearly that baby dolls lose their appeal when there is a real baby to snuggle and love. These realizations had been part of my thinking since the beginning of our family life and had played a role in our not doing school. Moreover, I never had liked grades and testing, so the next step toward unschooling was already in place.

The day came to tell my husband that we needed to have a talk about my changing educational philosophy. After hemming and hawing, I finally said the word: *unschooling*. "I knew that," he readily replied. I was stunned. How could he know something that I still hadn't wrapped my mind around?

My husband helped me to see the importance of education coming out of real experiences. God created us to know, love, and serve Him. God also created an environment in which these things can happen. He places the infant in his mother's arms, and as those baby eyes gaze up into the loving eyes of the mother, he learns about the love God has for him. It is both a great responsibility and a wonderful gift, a gift that has left me breathless with joy each time I have nursed my brand-new babes.

God has given each of us a unique personality, and in His infinite wisdom, God then calls us each to fulfill a particular plan. While I do have responsibilities regarding the education of my children, I judge that the discernment of God's plan for each of them belongs primarily to them. I need to give them both the freedom and the resources to discover their calling.

Countless conversations with my sister Sabine have also played a role in the way we live and learn together. I bounce ideas off her and the Holy Spirit on a regular basis; that helps to keep panic at bay. It appears that quite a large percentage of the population is concerned that homeschooling in general and unschooling specifically will leave giant voids in a child's education. "How do you know that you haven't missed something?" and "When do you decide that they're done?" are two frequent queries. Internally I quip that I'll go over them with a fine-tooth comb and pop a thermometer into their mouths, but externally I smile and say, "Of course we'll leave gaps—we must leave room for everything else that they'll desire to learn. As for being done, we're never done learning, are we? If you mean ready for college, that's up to them to discern, with our help and guidance of course."

In our home, unschooling means living life with all its ups and downs, joys and sorrows. As a Catholic family we live the liturgical year, which is then reflected in our activities and learning. We are in relationships with one another and with Christ, and the things we do spring out of those relationships. We are not perfect, and we all have strong, passionate personalities. But one day at a time, we live and learn together, and by His grace we grow ever closer to our heavenly Father.

CHAPTER NINE

Sabine's Family: The Path Intended

Sabine and her husband are now the parents of eight children. Although homeschooling was not their original path, she and her husband knew their third child would not do well in a school setting, and so the adventure began. Their oldest, a daughter, is now married and the mother of a little boy; she is Sabine's greatest affirmation of unschooling.

The family's life changed dramatically on October 15, 2008, when their almost two-year-old son, Michael, was involved in a near-drowning accident; he now requires full-time care at home. The family lives out Christ's commandment to love one another in their day to day care of Michaelman. Sabine writes about Michael at his CaringBridge website: www.caringbridge.org/visit/lovemichael.

The chief need of the child is to experience love . . .

—Dr. Herbert Ratner, *Nature, the Physician, and the Family*

"Do you know what you did to me?"

"What?" I asked with some trepidation. In fact, I was close to being defensive.

"I'm a freak!" answered my eighteen-year-old daughter, "I love my class! I love history!"

It was her first college class, the first classroom she had sat in since she finished her fourth grade year in public school. Although she knew that her friends in high school had not enjoyed most of their schooling, she was surprised at how openly her college peers despised the very idea of sitting through another history course. They were simply unwilling to believe that learning could be exciting and enjoyable.

Many times during the last nine years of homeschooling our children, I have wondered if we were on the right road. My daughter's enthusiasm for learning and her desire to share her experience with me confirmed that I have been following the path intended for me and my children.

I am Sabine, wife to Bill and mom to seven children, aged nineteen to two years old, and sister to Beate. Our homeschooling odyssey began in the fall of 1999 when our third child was about to begin kindergarten. My husband and I knew school wouldn't be a good fit for Jacob. His two older sisters were in school (fourth and second grades) and while they did well, there were things about their school experience we didn't like. So we kept Jacob home. I loosely "did school" for about six weeks that first year, then life took over and Jacob learned anyway.

The next year I would have sent him to the same school the girls were in, but I couldn't get the in-district transfer. Then the girls said they'd like to try homeschooling. Given how much I thought they liked school, I had no idea they would never want to go back.

That first year with all three at home I bought some curricula, and we used it very little. We read a lot and talked a lot—and didn't realize that what we were doing was called unschooling. As it turns out, we have never stuck to any curriculum for very long—as in hours, not days, weeks, or months! The kids occasionally pick up and work with various curricula, but the learning seems to occur more smoothly when it's on their terms.

Sometime during that year when our girls decided to stay home, my sister got on the Internet for the first time and discovered an email list of Catholic homeschoolers who followed the ideas of Charlotte Mason. We found much inspiration on that list. I loved the book suggestions we found there, and Charlotte's methods of copywork, dictation, and narration fit very naturally into our life.

Since then Charlotte Mason has taken a back seat to radical unschooling, and our children have been subjected to my efforts to try to inspire them in a variety of ways. I am learning to trust in their ability to learn through the course of our life, although I continue to sometimes struggle with my own failures and lack of motivation.

Unschooling in our home often looks pretty relaxed, but that doesn't mean we aren't busy—or that we aren't learning. We take day trips; we spend time with my sister and her family at their home across the street, with horses and a steady stream of hot or iced coffee. The kids and their cousins come up with all sorts of activities to keep them occupied and learning.

In the summertime my husband has extra work, building pipe fences and drilling fence post holes. Here in the Texas Hill Country a rock auger is required to fix fence posts in the ground unless you have a couple of hours and lots of muscle to spend on every hole. At nearly fifteen, our oldest son can do a lot of the physical work his dad can do. Every job we go to, people tell us how surprising it is to see a young teenager doing that kind of intense physical labor—and enjoying his work.

When we spend time online, the kids usually do so in pairs, playing games, updating MySpace, and visiting blogs. My time on the Internet is usually spent reading apologetics and Catholic/political blogs. We go to the library at least once a week and bring home books, books on tape and CD, and DVDs. I don't enjoy reading aloud, but my children love me to, and so I do, though picture books are read aloud much more frequently than longer books. We all enjoy listening to chapter books on audio together.

As for TV and movies, we often have unrestricted TV, but the environment is not unrestricted. I've locked many channels, and while the teens know the password, I have never known them to abuse their privilege. They encourage each other, and they enjoy having a good relationship with me. Also my husband and I have been very careful when it comes to the programs we view with them.

While an unschooler who is not Catholic may feel comfortable letting a teen experiment with movies or even with risky behavior, as Catholics we do not consider immoral choices acceptable. Our freedom of choice is meant to be exercised within the confines of a set of definite values. Our children belong to God first, and we have certain obligations due to that.

Oddly enough, after years at home and after being our impetus for beginning to unschool, Jacob decided he would like to try public school. He entered two years ago as a seventh grader. Although school was very different from what he was used to at home, he enjoyed it and had no trouble keeping up with his classmates. I was quite worried about what he would be exposed to from his peers, and not too worried about the teaching philosophies. As it turned out, the kids he chose to hang out with were fine, and no worrisome behavior issues arose. But the school itself? The things I had hated when the girls were in school came flooding back to me, and I found myself filled with a sense of hostility toward the way things are done there. Still, I stood back and let Jacob go.

Going to school for the first time at almost thirteen years of age, Jacob did struggle a little for about six weeks. Once he got the hang of the terminology and how to do the work, he flew through the next two years fairly easily. Educationally (and socially) he did fine, although we had made no attempt previously to cover what school kids were covering—in fact, we had barely done any textbook work at all. The two years prior to his entering school we were caught up in radical unschooling, and yet the kids did learn.

Does all of this mean I never question our unschooling way? I must admit that I often feel less than confident about it. I thought this feeling would pass, but maybe it is part of who I am, and maybe it is not that unusual. I still have moments of panic about how it will all come together, but then I think about what is most important to me, namely, the Faith and our family relationships. If my children find themselves on solid footing in regard to these, I'm sure the rest will fall into place. Even in the world of work, employers look for people who are trustworthy, reliable, and willing to work hard. A strong faith and healthy relationships will help our children be just such people.

Once children are school aged, we can easily become afraid that without all the formal schooling we ourselves had, our children will be short-changed. I had the mistaken belief that scope and sequence were some sort of holy grail of a well-rounded education. I am lucky to have the sister I do. She was trained as a teacher but has always held an unschool-friendly philosophy, which her university classes supported. She was (and is) a very dedicated early childhood educator who discovered unschooling when teaching in the kindergarten classroom and before the term was popular. Her professional knowledge combined with her personal wisdom has helped to take the mystique out of scope and sequence. You might say that one-size-fits-all never fits anyone very well.

This lesson has been further borne out in my home, where each of my children is free to learn according to his or her own timing. For example, I have children who learned to read at a young age, and then there are those children who came to it later. But I have stopped thinking in terms of *ahead* and *behind*. I call this the compare-your-kids-to-others monster and it is amazing, no matter how great kids are, mothers seem to have to battle this beast. Fight it off we must. It is a very destructive habit which, as far as I can see, only brings trouble.

If the child is a bit "behind" the curve, comparison breeds negative feelings toward him or her. We begin to ask ourselves, *Why can't they just get this?* These feelings don't help us help the child, but rather they frustrate us, and we in turn frustrate the child. If the children are "ahead," prideful feelings develop.

So slay the monster! Remember that the most important consideration is that the children continue to enjoy learning and not believe there is something wrong with them when it takes time, even years, to master important skills.

Math is another area in which we have let go of a comparative approach. My way of thinking about the acquisition of math skills has changed, and I no longer look at grade levels in the same way. So many arithmetic concepts are supposed to be taught in early grade levels by spending year after year trying to do essentially the same things. But I have seen that these concepts come much more quickly if we wait for the child to have lots of exposure to real life situations such as sorting, counting, seeing amounts, cooking, spending, and the like.

Consequently, we have had a very eclectic approach to math—no drills, just applying it in everyday life. We engage in plenty of hands-on activities with our young children, and play all kinds of games: board games, card games, dominoes, and so on. Again I recall Jacob's experience entering seventh grade. He was surprised that he wasn't behind on the school's schedule of learning and knowledge, and he did fine in math as well as the other subjects.

What about when the children become teenagers? I have found my teens are inspired, and no less motivated to learn than young children. They realize that knowing how to write well is an important part of becoming an adult who communicates effectively. They see the necessity of some higher math skills, and have chosen to work with textbooks, using them as a spine for concepts they would like to clarify and have a handle on for college entrance exams. When reading, writing, and learning are central parts of Mom or Dad's life, naturally the teens will see them as good things. If we believe that young children can be successfully unschooled and learn the things they need to know, why would we believe otherwise regarding teens?

About two years ago a friend mentioned to me that during the first two years of high school the teens can have total freedom regarding what to study, and the unschooling parent doesn't have to worry. Then the last two years will naturally be more focused on what the teens need to do to move forward with their adult lives. This approach worked out well with my oldest daughter, and lo and behold my next daughter's high school years are following a similar pattern.

I have required nothing of my sixteen-year-old these past two years. She blogs frequently, reads daily, talks sometimes incessantly (but never too much), is active in her church youth group (which required a written personal testimony), takes care of siblings, cooks, cleans, and is simply engaged in living. Now that her older sister and more of their friends have started college, she too is looking at what she wants to do, where she wants to go, and how she can get there. She is choosing resources at home and is charting a course. Textbooks are part of the game plan for her, but I am not worried about their ruining her love of learning, for by now that is very well established.

Sometimes I have been asked whether unschooling—in particular my not requiring the children to do schoolwork—will prevent my children from developing the ability to work hard and stick to a task. How will they learn that sometimes they have to obey? Is it even Christian to give this much freedom to our children? I am always surprised when parents believe that making kids do schoolwork, or punishing them for not getting it done, will teach them discipline and other virtues.

In answering these concerns, I like to ask some questions of my own. Isn't it likely that even in an unschooling home we will ask our children to do certain things they consider unpleasant? For example, don't we ask our children to hold a crying younger sibling? Or play with the toddler so we can cook, even though they would rather finish their computer game or story? I have found through the years that in virtue of being an active member of a busy family, large or small, each child will have an assortment of tasks that have to be done. In order for the family to function, things have to be taken care of. Just because we don't put learning into that category doesn't mean the children cannot or will not learn to be disciplined individuals with a desire to accomplish goals and to work hard. I have even seen that the more we simply focus on the desire to learn in young children, the more the desire for some rigorous academics develops in their teen years.

A couple of years ago I had an epiphany regarding this issue of self-discipline and my eldest daughter. I hadn't required any academics. She imposed work on herself and checked into what she needed to do to get where she wanted to go. Still, I was wondering if I had missed the boat on that stick-to-it-iveness that we all value, and value for good reason. Then I thought about our struggles with her horse.

Several years before, she had been given a horse by her aunt, because my daughter and the horse had such a beautiful bond. She made various plans, which included showing the horse and breeding it. Then after the horse was bred, it had a severe reaction to a pesticide. The vet mishandled the horse, which resulted in four cracked vertebrae and a severe laceration to the animal's head, but the horse survived, even sustaining pregnancy through the trauma. I saw my daughter take incredible care of this horse, nurturing it and working for its recovery even though her favorite part of having a horse—the riding—was gone. I realized that my daughter was sticking with it when it really mattered. She showed us that when she needs to do something, even something that is not fun or something that requires selflessness, she definitely has it in her to follow through.

How does our Faith fit into the picture? I am convinced that our Faith is best internalized through unschooling. I see that in a society like ours it is especially important to have adequate knowledge of our religion so we can defend and explain it, and yet I believe that when it comes to passing on the Faith to our children, the best thing we can do is model it for them. We let them see us praying for them and others, asking for forgiveness when we've made mistakes, inviting them to pray and allowing them to accept or decline the invitation. With my own kids, my living out my faith in a genuine way leads them, as they get older, to a greater acceptance of the Faith and a stronger desire to live it.

Sharing our love of the Mass is a great example of how and why unschooling works. A good lady I know once made a wonderful comparison; she likened learning to love the Mass to learning to love the symphony. Children won't learn to love the symphony by being forced to attend and to sit still and to "appreciate" the music. Instead, exposing them to the music you love, talking about the instruments, and teaching them about great composers is much more likely to get them interested and to develop in them the same love for music that you have.

Mass is just like that. If a parent truly loves the Mass and believes it is heaven on earth, the children can't help but fall in love with it too. Just like the symphony, however, having daily Mass attendance forced probably will not help the children develop the love for God that is already written on their hearts. When we totally fall in love with Jesus, then we want to spend time with Him, and we want to learn about His Church.

I strongly believe that God deliberately put each of us into this time and place. We have lots of opportunities that those in the past didn't. And yet we are on shaky ground thinking that we can create utopia if we just do everything by the book. We do live in a fallen world, and sin exists.

My family has found that the secret to living virtuously and learning happily at home with a large family is to be very, very flexible. I've given up on the idea that everything will get done every day. Even if I had fewer kids, I would probably not get everything done. But as we go with the flow, I trust that this flexibility will be an advantage for the children later on in life. It is crucial for us to be close to our children now; that is the heart of the matter. Respecting the child is the underlying foundation of unschooling, and for us, unschooling is the path we were meant to take.

CHAPTER TEN

Susan's Family: Life is the Lesson

Susan grew up in southwest Ohio, and now lives in Kentucky with her husband, Joseph, and their five children aged four through seventeen. Twelve years ago, after their oldest child "graduated" kindergarten, the family commenced their lives without schooling. Susan has a B.A. in psychology from Thomas More College in Crestview Hills, Kentucky, and had the privilege to serve families as a social worker for twelve years. Her experiences included geriatrics, home care, dementia care, and hospice. Susan and her family continue to love life and learning while they seek to live simply and joyfully without school.

Love God first, and do as you will.

—St. Augustine, "Sermon on the Epistle of St. John"

As many parents do, I began to think about education when my oldest child started preschool. The classroom environment was fun and exciting, and the director energetically proclaimed that we didn't need to worry about the children learning: they would learn through play. We happily enrolled our second daughter in preschool as well when she reached the ripe age of three. I would have waited until she was four, but her two best friends and neighbors were going to attend, and I hoped to encourage those young relationships. This sound beginning seemed the way to go, because "that's just what parents do nowadays." I was to some extent going along with the crowd, but even then I was aware of a small inner voice whispering questions, wondering if this was a little early, asking why we make these choices to send our little ones away from home for education.

Both my husband and I had grown up with Catholic schooling, elementary through college. The parochial school looked like the natural next step for our daughters although the preschool teacher, a Catholic mom whose kids went to the Catholic school, suggested that we send our older daughter to the public school after kindergarten. "It's more fun," she explained, "more active; the Catholic school is more 'sit in your seat, be still' . . . academic." She spoke the word *academic* in a tone of dismay. Despite her advice, tradition initially won out for us as it apparently had for her, and we sent our daughter to the Catholic school.

At this time I was working outside the home, but homeschooling was constantly knocking on my consciousness, at first as an unwelcome guest, then in a more appealing form. A man I worked with had a homeschooling family. He was a nice man, but I was not attracted by the description of his wife being the teacher at the dining room table. Next I got involved with a book company that sold books through home shows, and I began to meet homeschooling families. Again, I was not impressed; in fact, I thought these people were slightly strange.

Soon, however, my image of homeschoolers started to change. I met a fellow book consultant who did not send her kids to school. This mother was intelligent and had a great relationship with her children, who were pleasant to be around. They read and learned and had a house full of projects and fun. Then my family doctor told me that he and his wife, also a doctor, had decided to homeschool their children—I was impressed. Finally, I met a woman from rural Indiana with a large family and some grown kids. She radiated a peace and confidence about her family. I realized that was what I wanted when it was my turn to look back, my children grown up. I was meeting people I liked and admired, who were intelligent . . . and who were homeschooling.

I decided to investigate homeschooling in a more thorough and direct manner, even though I wasn't ready to think about it as an option for our family. I immersed myself in books about education. I began by exploring classical homeschooling because our family doctor was working with Laura Berquist, whose program seemed ideal in some ways. Laura was an experienced homeschooling parent and Catholic, both of which were important to me. Although I enjoyed *Designing Your Own Classical Curriculum*, and hoped to have my children become well versed in Latin, logic, rhetoric and the other aspects of classical education, I felt a little intimidated, not having that background myself.

I first heard about unschooling through the book consultant supervisor, who introduced me to an online unschooling discussion group. The conversations I encountered were both lively and down to earth, not simply idealistic. Sandra Dodd, the apparent leader, could cause intense friction. The participants were saying, "Question your thinking, it developed from schooling. Question whether you are living with the belief that children learn naturally, or whether you are trying to impose your own desired outcomes." When the discussions ignited my anger, I knew I needed to take a step back and reconsider my assumptions.

I began to read John Holt's books, and soon I was hooked. His books *Teach Your Own*, *How Children Learn* and *How Children Fail* delighted me, and when I discovered his newsletter *Growing Without Schooling*, I reveled in the stories of real people joyfully keeping their children out of school. I continued to research homeschooling in general, but unschooling held a particular attraction for me.

Amid all my research, I found out I was pregnant with our third child, and my husband and I had even more to consider. We jointly decided that I would take an early career retirement, so that I could devote my full attention to our growing family.

I resigned from my job, then I had the baby, and we wondered how to make ends meet. My husband and I went out one evening to discuss the many changes in our family's life. The homeschool topic was on our agenda, and as we sat and talked, I went over with my husband what I had learned. He listened and then said definitively, "You need to do it."

I was shocked. I had supposed he would reject the homeschooling option straight off, sure he would want to simply continue with traditional Catholic schooling for the children. Instead, he responded, "If only you could see your own face." He was sure homeschooling was the right thing for us because I lit up when I talked about it. It was a rare moment, and I felt it must be the work of the Holy Spirit. On a more practical note, we figured we couldn't really mess up much for first grade anyway, and we could reevaluate the next summer and see where to go from there. So we began.

Along with lots of other new homeschoolers, I attended a homeschool curriculum fair and sale. There I met quite a few teachers and former teachers who had determined that school was not the place for learning. Despite their profession, they would not be sending their own children to school. I looked at regular school-at-home curricula, but found them mostly dry and uninspiring. Plus I had a hard time imagining sitting in our version of a one-room schoolhouse with my six-year-old, while playing with her three-year-old sister and caring for an infant who wasn't sleeping well.

As our homeschooling began in earnest, I immediately experienced challenges from both internal and external forces. I became aware of the deeply entrenched views on learning that I had internalized through my own schooling, and next to these I saw the cultural norms and expectations I had absorbed over the years. Despite my attraction to unschooling, I remained full of concerns about controlling the outcome of the childrens' education. The many questions I still had and the competing ideas filling my mind all boiled down to one concern: Could I truly believe that children would learn naturally? Externally, I cultivated a life of joy and freedom at home with my children, yet society continued to demand that I send them off to the experts. The growing homeschool community provided some refuge from the voices inside and outside my mind, but the respite was by no means complete. In the homeschooling circles I was part of, almost everyone denounced and ridiculed unschooling.

During our first years without school, as I gradually grew to understand unschooling better, I began to sort out the tangle of opposing thoughts with which I struggled. I finally acknowledged that unschooling seemed terrific, as long as my children were geniuses; I still wanted them to meet my expectations for academic success. I wanted to live the unschooling principles, but when it came right down to it, I frequently doubted whether unschooling ideals could actually work.

Imagine my angst as a concerned mother: I wasn't only concerned about school subjects (though such anxiety did loom large), I was also hoping and fearing what would come from my seeing such areas as chores and even food through the lens of unschooling. Regarding chores, would my children ever learn to contribute to our household if I didn't require specific chores, or particular times to do those chores? In the area of food, would my children really eat nutritional food if they had their choice?

But most importantly, I wanted my children to read, early and up to my expectations. I have always been a voracious reader, and reading has served me well. I found it natural to follow the common advice about reading to my children. My first daughter loved this time, my second daughter would rarely sit still for a read aloud, but in both cases, I didn't see the results I desired. When my oldest didn't read by age six, I began to wonder what was wrong. Upon reflection, I realized that my anxious tone was obvious to my daughter, despite my attempt to rid myself of it. She seemed aware that she wasn't living up to what I wanted of her, and she reacted as any normal child would—by believing she was the source of my frustrations about her reading. While I sought to help her, my attitude was setting obstacles in her path.

We had barely begun, and I already had to step back and fortify myself. My desire to control blocked me from actually unschooling. It cannot be something that occurs in your mind; it can only happen by living in each particular moment, with each unique child. I needed to get past my doubts, or at least do a better job of keeping them to myself. The online discussion groups became a helpful outlet, and I continued to research. Raymond and Dorothy Moore's *Better Late than Early* proved pivotal in developing my understanding about children learning to read. Stories of late readers convinced me that children do grow into literate beings, loving reading and reading well, but first comes the desire, and children will desire to read in their own time. I saw that people learn in various ways, and according to their own unique timetable. Our project shifted from homeschooling to unschooling as I began trusting my children to figure out when they were ready to learn. My job became simpler; instead of teaching them this or that, my role became to instill confidence in the children.

In our second year at home, we joined a homeschooling co-op, but it was very schooly, and in conflict with the ideas I was trying to integrate. When I attended group events, the conversations with new acquaintances centered on curricula. After giving my pat response, "We pull from lots of sources," I usually had nothing more to say, and furthermore, I wasn't happy about what I was likely to hear from the other mothers. Sometimes the education going on in their homes seemed much more about the parents' expectations and goals than about the children, and other times I went away afraid that maybe I wouldn't be able to provide my children with what they needed.

Eventually, we discovered a group of homeschoolers who met once weekly at a gymnasium for group games and physical activities. The group allowed us to connect with other families and develop a sense of community. For the most part, I remained quiet about our unschooling approach, especially when unschooling came up more generally in conversation and I heard it met with disdain. As my experience with my children increased and I gained more confidence about my choices, I learned to express my point of view occasionally, although I never did become completely forthright.

Over the years, a few of the women from the group have approached me privately about unschooling, either out of curiosity, or because they are struggling. I have heard women say that they would love to unschool, because then they could do nothing and let the kids have a free-for-all. "How simple to sit around and do whatever I want and let the kids go," they remark. These moms think unschooling (which they equate with ignoring the children) would be especially helpful when they feel tired, or are busy with a new baby or another life event that interferes with their curriculum plans.

In fact, my experience has been quite the opposite. The periods of life transition have caused me to wonder if it might not be a good idea to find some curriculum materials to anchor everyone. Maybe all of us are just looking for an easier way to manage all of our responsibilities during our trials. My challenge has been that I feel disengaged from the children during such times, yet as our unschooling has developed, I have learned that life is the lesson. Integrating every type of experience, the painful as well as the pleasant, the difficult as well as the easy, is part of our education. Lessons in character and virtue, humility and human nature, frequently come from these very situations which I had originally considered interruptions to our learning.

Over the years I have noticed that those who subscribe to the philosophy of learning in freedom can end up feeling isolated. Community is a vital aspect of growing and understanding, but from the outset our choices put us at odds with others and cause them discomfort. For example, one day we were at a park and saw a family we used to live near, and we invited them to come to our home. The mother declined the offer. I was puzzled but felt comfortable enough to ask why; she explained her concern that her children would see that some people don't have to go to school, and they would beg her to allow them that choice. She said that she would not be able to consider it because she and her husband both worked.

Another uncomfortable situation arose when my daughter made friends with a girl her age who had recently moved to the neighborhood. At first everything went well; they played together and were friends for about a year, until the girl went to kindergarten. About a week before school started, my daughter and I walked over to see if our neighbor could play. The mother came out and approached my five-year-old daughter with the declaration, "Sylvia won't be available to play with you anymore since she will be starting school next week." She never even said anything to me. Needless to say, my daughter was upset. I was stunned myself—kindergarten was only three hours a day on weekdays. But the mother kept her word, and her daughter was not available even on off days or school vacations. It was heartbreaking, but I realized that this mother had spent much of the summer convincing her daughter that it is good to go to school, and it is what every five-year-old does. She couldn't risk having her daughter see that this wasn't universally true.

I have mentioned the difficulties we've had as unschoolers among more formal homeschoolers, and also the conflicts that can arise between my homeschooling family and families whose children go to school. But even among unschoolers I have felt odd, because Catholics are few and far between among us, and formal religion is not acceptable to many who unschool. I have little in common with the few unschoolers I have met, so our paths seldom cross. Unschooling itself might provide common ground for adults exploring the ideas, but otherwise, each family remains unique. Fortunately, fellow Catholic unschoolers have found each other on online discussion lists and have developed a Yahoo group called Unschooling Catholics. Like-minded women I have met in this group offer one another a wealth of encouragement and knowledge, as well as prayer support, and are helping me to form my own faith. In a sometimes hostile world, the Internet has been a wonderful place to find affirmation in each other and in our common creed.

The silver lining of the external challenges eventually shone out brightly. In facing the misperceptions and misunderstandings of the label *unschooler*, I have learned to listen with an open mind and heart. I have discovered that parents desire good for their children. Unschooling surely isn't for everyone. As I've become aware of my guardedness about it, I've realized that I wanted to impose understanding on others, rather than accept them and let them find their own best educational methods. I eventually saw that for me school-at-home or traditional school is likely to cause problems with my integrity and barriers in my relationships with my children, but there are people who manage to maintain good relationships with their children while choosing these options.

I now appreciate the differences in how parents can express their love for their children. After I had integrated the unschooling principles more deeply and worked past feeling defensive, I could bridge relationships with others who were making different choices. Also, I grew in confidence as I watched my children explore and learn naturally.

By the time *Homeschooling with Gentleness* came along, I was much more comfortable living and loving our family life. I did feel a twinge of envy at the picture of Suzie's son reading prodigiously, and beyond that initial response, I wondered what it would be like to be able to give that kind of time to a child without having to balance the needs of infants and toddlers. Unschooling can require great attention and energy to create a rich atmosphere and to support the interests and dreams of each and every child.

With a larger family, this constellation of goals can feel overwhelming to me. I admit that on more than one occasion I have been "gentleness challenged" as our family has grown and changed. And unschooling with a larger family presents some practical predicaments. How to inspire, encourage, provide opportunity, and develop the passions of children who have diverging interests? To strew a path, as unschoolers recommend, there must be a pathway, but with seven in the house, there are days when having a pathway is as good as it gets! The energy to strew interesting items along it has not always been there.

Early in our marriage, my husband and I met an older Irish couple at church. This lovely woman and her husband had reared twelve children, and we often chatted and laughed about large family life. When I asked how they managed, she said that with each child their faith grew, and she had to depend more on God. Although we have only five children, I must agree with her assessment. Meeting my human limits reminds me that I need to rely fully on God. I grow in trust that it is God who has the big picture in mind. That families come in varying sizes is a blessing, each size providing its own particular gifts.

I have come to believe that if I want to happily unschool, my life needs to be the example. I hope to follow St. Francis's suggestion of preaching the gospel always, using words only when necessary.

To illustrate, several years ago I became aware of my anxiety over my children not writing much. I realized they didn't see me ever write more than a grocery list or a check; I usually e-mailed before they were awake or after they were in bed, and I wasn't sure they would realize that I was writing even if they were watching me. After I thought about writing and how I value it, I volunteered to work on the parish newsletter. I was hoping that even if I didn't write much for it, my children would be exposed to other people writing in order to communicate. I enjoyed the work, and some of the children joined me in my enthusiasm, though their participation was more in the folding, labeling, and mailing areas.

As can happen when one is thinking and praying about something specific, a further opportunity arose. I had the chance to work on a more substantial writing endeavor, editing for a friend. This work lasted months and brought me great pleasure. I was also gratified that my passion for writing had become more central in my life, and more visible to my family.

Last year my older three children began publishing a monthly newsletter. It included poems and cartoons, interviews and reports. We had fun with it, and then let it go when interest faded. I notice more writing around our home—in notes, letters, journals; it was not required, and no pressure was brought to bear. The children managed well with writing deadlines, too, as they chose to be involved in some projects that required reports. I don't claim the credit, but I rejoice that the children saw that I loved writing, and that writing enriched our family and communal life. They observed me as I learned about writing, layout, editing, and mailing. They got to live with someone who found joy in this kind of work. I hope that's what they remember: the gratification of work, learning, taking responsibility, extending a helping hand.

My real work has now become the weeding of my own soul; it takes years, with both new weeds and old familiar ones cropping up periodically. Recently, for example, I have been thinking about my oldest daughter going to college. Some of my concern arises from constantly fielding the questions of others regarding her plans. According to the school community, she is now a junior in high school and should take the ACT and SAT tests. She should begin to look at colleges and visit them; she should begin the process of determining her career; she should be getting a job to earn money. When these questions arise, I have to remind myself that the reality is that my daughter *could* take the tests, visit the campuses, and so on—but while I know she is a good candidate for college, the choice is hers. My daughter certainly will continue her education in life, but she herself will find the best ways to do so.

All the challenges, internal, external, and practical have paved the way for my growth in trust and humility. It is a journey inward, as I consider whether my life truly reflects what I hold dear. I have moved from "I should teach the children . . ." to "I should offer them resources for . . ." and even further to "I will offer resources and information as I am able." I have given up the notion that I can (or ought to) control who they become, as well as the notion that I am ultimately responsible for their choices. It has taken me time to see that learning is secondary to living well, or at least only one integral part of living well, rather than something that precedes living. We have found that unschooling is not merely about a child's education at home—but also about that child's life, today, tomorrow, and always. For us it has started at home, in the early years, but it doesn't stop there. Life, after all, is the lesson.

PART THREE

More Catholic Unschoolers

CHAPTER ELEVEN

Intermisson: Why More?

Take what you like, and leave the rest.

—12-Step Program saying

As we begin Part Three of this book, I have already had the pleasure of introducing to you several of my unschooling friends. Get ready to meet more wonderful women and their families, but first, while they wait in the wings, I would like to explain why they are here.

One of the reasons I wrote *Homeschooling with Gentleness* was that I had reached the point where reading homeschooling books frustrated me. I was looking for someone to tell my story, someone who had a temperament like mine, a life like mine, or at least a homeschooling style like mine. I realized that if I intended to keep reading about education, I needed to write the book I wanted to read. I didn't know if there were any other unschooling Catholics in the world, but I knew I was one, and I thought that if there were a half dozen more somewhere out there, my book might encourage them too.

Times have changed, and I am only thinking of the last seven years. My first book has sold over a thousand copies, which makes me think there are a lot more Catholic unschoolers than I had suspected, or than there used to be. The growth of the Internet has also made it easier for like-minded women to connect with and support one another. These days I belong to a Yahoo group of unschooling Catholics that has over two hundred members.

I decided to put together *A Little Way of Homeschooling* because, as useful as the Internet can be, it is no substitute for a book. Knowing of so many more Catholic unschoolers, I wanted to collect their experiences into one bound volume. Again, my motive was two-fold. A new book would give me another book to read about homeschooling, and also provide inspiration and reassurance to others.

Whereas the Internet easily has room for hundreds of Catholic unschoolers, the confines of a single book limit me to far fewer. Nonetheless, I wanted to bring together as wide a variety of Catholic unschoolers as possible. This is where more Catholic unschoolers come in.

Why more? You have met eight Catholic unschooling families in addition to mine. Isn't that enough to give you a generous smattering of types, a wide array of examples? In a word: no. If our little way of homeschooling were to end here, you would be left with the impression we so often receive, and you might go back to your life with the attitude we too frequently adopt, namely, that it's all or nothing—in this case, with regard to unschooling.

Not entirely convinced that unschooling is a perfect fit for your family? Maybe you will want to follow the ladies in the next four chapters. They imitate the great educator St. John Bosco who, as his biographers describe him, "was not concerned with any one educational idea; he chose what he thought useful for his purposes and imprinted on them his own particular style" (*Educational Philosophy of St. John Bosco*, 55).

In the upcoming chapters, we offer you something more than pure unschooling. There are more families here to illustrate some of the many more ways Catholics can learn at home. You will be meeting four women who are creative and funny, and who have discovered interesting ways to integrate elements of unschooling with more formal approaches to learning. There will be more reflections and more anecdotes to show that unschooling (and any educational method) need not be an all or nothing endeavor.

St. Thérèse tells us about God, "How delicately considerate He is, and pleased with even little" (*Spirit of St. Thérèse*, 5). Yes, He is so delicately considerate, so tender in His concern for each of us, that He has in mind plans for our peace long before we have discovered them. I hope the women you read about convey to you that sweet touch of His, that unique plan He has for each family.

Perhaps you have seen a glimpse of your family life in the preceding pages, or maybe you will find your match in the pages that follow. Possibly you will identify with individual pieces of chapters, while beginning to see that the completed puzzle of your family's life and learning will portray a picture uniquely your own. Whichever it is, keep in mind the second part of St. Thérèse's saying, that He is pleased with even little.

Try not to be discouraged if you are still searching for the best way for your family, or if you are happy with your way but frustrated with the slow progress. After all, traveling with children always takes more time than we anticipate. Remember that Jesus is satisfied with even little, and then follow the advice in Psalm 34: "Look to Him, and be radiant; so your faces shall never be ashamed." You are doing what you can to bring your children to God; rejoice in that. Rejoice in the time you have together, and be assured that Jesus is pleased with your efforts.

As you continue to walk with us along our little way of Catholic unschooling, we are going to direct your attention to some of the intriguing byways that branch off the main path. Feel free to wander and explore; may the angels go with you.

CHAPTER TWELVE

Karen's Family: The Unschooling Equation

Karen Edmisten and her husband have three girls, ranging from elementary-school age to high-school age. The family lives in Nebraska, where Karen homeschools the girls and writes as often as time and mothering allow. Karen is the author of The Rosary, Keeping Company with Jesus and Mary *(Servant Books, 2009), and* Through the Year with Mary *(Servant, 2010), a compendium of quotations on the Blessed Mother. Find her online at www.karenedmisten.com.*

Be not afraid!

—Pope John Paul II, *Crossing the Threshold of Hope*

Recently, we had a new priest from our parish over for dinner. Knowing that we homeschool, he asked, "So, do you have a classroom set up?"

I laughed. "No, we're all over the place! The kitchen, the living room, or we snuggle up together on my bed to read. We're everywhere."

When I thought about it later, I realized that "we're everywhere" fits more than merely our physical location. We are indeed everywhere in terms of both *where* we educate, and *how* we educate. I can't pin down our classroom coordinates, and I can't give our method a specific label.

I think of our family as unschoolers, or at least on the fringe of unschooling. I chat blithely with friends about investigating interests, shoring up strengths, and immersing ourselves passionately in current obsessions, and of how these result in gobs of learning. If we aren't the truest of unschoolers, we certainly lean that way.

But then, something begins to possess me. It starts around May or June and accelerates as the summer unfolds. What happens? I begin to plan. And I blame it on the siren song of the catalogs.

First, it's only a little publication or two, straggling in with the mail, tucked in among bills and credit card offers. I try to be nonchalant, but then another appears, slightly more enticing than the first. I peek inside. I wonder if, perhaps, I should order just that one special something. Before I know it, I've received an unnaturally thick catalog that is formidable both in size and potential dollars spent. Yet somehow I'm feeling exhilarated; I can't wait to dig in. No amount of beeswax in the ears can keep me from this temptation. I crave a rendezvous with that stack of sheer potential. I wait for a quiet afternoon when everyone's out of the house, and I can curl up with a cup of coffee and my catalog tower. I'll savor every flick of the page and every possible purchase as I plot, dream, and anticipate the boxes that will arrive, brimming with crisp, clean promises.

I'm there. I'm immersed in CurricuLand. And somehow I've once again become the Planning Unschooler. The Unschooler with a Plan. To say, "I lean toward unschooling" but then add, "And here's how I plan" sounds as if I don't understand the philosophy, doesn't it? Am I un-unschooling? No, not really. It's just this crazy new math, and I indulge in it every year. Because for me, unschooling is simply the solution to the following equation:

My kids + books and plans + discussion (– boxed curriculum)
+ flexibility (– a rigid definition of education)
+ willingness to abandon plans = Unschooling

The beauty of homeschooling is that we get to do what works for us. Sometimes that means a carefully crafted plan. Other times, it means letting go of the plan to see where our days take us. Unschooling doesn't necessarily mean there's never a structured lesson, or never anything that looks like school, though it often means that. It doesn't mean we'll never touch a textbook or do a worksheet. If those things help, and learning happens, we sometimes do them. What unschooling means to me is that we needn't adhere to a model of school that doesn't serve us.

My model involves both planning and the undoing of plans. I love to make plans. I love to imagine, dream and order new books. (I especially love to order new books). But I'm not irrevocably tied to my plans, because I've seen how easily they can come undone—by pregnancy, illness, a move, or simply a new passion. And I've seen that both life and learning go on, despite the undoing. God in His wisdom always provides.

In weaving together these seemingly disparate methods of planning and unschooling, somehow I've come up with a plan (which perhaps I'll abandon) that works for us. I've come to see my method as an organic thing which lives, breathes and grows. It can, should, does and will change, or it will die.

"Finally, brothers, whatever is true, whatever is honorable, whatever is just, whatever is pure, whatever is lovely, whatever is gracious, if there is any excellence and if there is anything worthy of praise, think about these things," says St. Paul to the Philippians (4:8).

Somewhere along the way, I realized what a truly worthwhile education means to me: I want to instill in my children a love of learning about all things true, good and beautiful. Our ultimate goal is to love the Lord with all our heart, soul and strength (Deuteronomy 6:5). That begins with learning about and embracing our Faith, and it ends up encompassing all the beauty and goodness God has given us.

School, for us then, is about all things. It's not about checking off boxes or completing enough workbooks to measure up to someone else's predetermined standard. School is life; life is school. They're connected. When we lose sight of that connection, school becomes disconnected from everything else, including from all things true, good, and beautiful. School, when it's nothing more than a series of exercises to complete, becomes "that thing to get out of the way" so we can get back to real living. But when school is connected to life, it becomes a way of life.

How does this unfold in the day-to-day of our homeschool? Here are a couple of examples of how my planning grew and changed into something new and different.

My Plan: Read Beautiful Picture Books to My Preschooler During Advent
Where the Plan Took Us: Getting to Know the Mother of God

One year during Advent I said to my youngest daughter, "We get to go to Mass, to celebrate Mary's Immaculate Conception!"

She replied, "Oh, yes! Mary—the ship! The rose!"

I realized that she was recalling the images of the Blessed Mother from Barbara Helen Berger's lovely book, *The Donkey's Dream*, which introduces children to traditional Marian imagery. We'd read the book only a couple of times, but my daughter loved it, and had absorbed much of it.

Literature, including picture books, allows us to absorb lessons by way of exposure to beautiful ideas that we can ponder and discuss, even with a four-year-old.

My Plan: Study World War II
Where the Plan Took Us: To Theology and Beyond

While reading historical fiction set during the war, we discussed the Holocaust. My then-ten-year-old said, "Mom, how could God let this happen? He's so good. He could have stopped it."

How does one explain the problem of evil to a child?

I began by telling her that she had asked an eternal question, a philosopher's question, a wonderful question. I said that people have lost their faith over that question when the answers seemed inadequate, elusive, or wrong. I took her back in time, to Adam and Eve, and asked what God gave them.

"A choice!" she said.

"Yes, a choice. He allowed them to choose good or bad, right or wrong, didn't He?"

"Yes."

"Why do you think He did that?"

"Hmm . . . I don't know. Wouldn't it be nicer if He'd made them obey?"

"Well, yes, in some ways, it would be nicer." (I reminded myself to explain *felix culpa* to her later.) "But let's think about what kind of a relationship comes out of making someone do something."

From there, we put on a little demonstration. What would it be like if my children were mere puppets I could control? What if I could manipulate their mouths and, ventriloquist like, throw my voice so that I could hear them say on command, "I love you, Mommy dear." Both of my older girls lapsed into fits of giggles as Lizzy played the puppet, mouthing the words. The demonstration made its point: puppets aren't capable of real love. For love to mean anything, it has to be freely given. Had God made us pliable puppets, our love for Him would be meaningless. I told the kids that they would read a similar (if more eloquent) explanation someday in C. S. Lewis's *Mere Christianity*. I summed it up this way:

"There's a world of difference between a puppet's artificial 'I love you,' and the feeling I get when one of you gives me a picture you've drawn, or a gift you've made, and it's something you've created purely out of love for me. That kind of 'I love you' is real, and means everything to me, because you've chosen to do it."

Then we talked about the freedom God gave human beings —our free will—allowing us to make choices about everything, including love. Where the possibility of true love exists, the possibility of utterly rejecting love co-exists. And where the possibility of rejecting love exists, there is the potential for evil. Some people will choose evil.

It's not a pat answer. Not even a very satisfying one most of the time, especially when our children are contemplating suffering. But it is the only answer that makes sense. And as for putting a stop to evil? I told them that's what God counts on us to do.

None of the above was in "the plan." Nowhere did I have lesson plans with "Discuss the problem of evil" penciled in for the day. The discussion grew, organically, from the book we read and the time I allowed for talking. Talking makes up most of our curriculum.

On a less serious note, I'm reminded of the time I taught my eldest daughter what the word *allusion* meant. She was quite young and we were reading a Clifford the Big Red Dog book in which there was a storm. As Emily Elizabeth worries about the tornado, we see, through a window, a woman riding a bicycle in the air.

"Just like in *The Wizard of Oz*!" my daughter exclaimed.

Delighted, I said, "Yes! When a writer deliberately reminds us of a scene from something else, it's called an allusion." The term stuck. And so I had a five-year-old asking things like, "Mommy, this book has a talking pig. Do you think that's an allusion to *Charlotte's Web*?"

A talking curriculum pays off. When my children are young, I begin pointing out connections between what we are reading and real life. I give the girls names and labels for those interesting, intricate ways in which ideas are woven together, build upon each other, and inspire new thoughts and connections. As they get older I encourage them to keep making connections, and soon, one happy day they start pointing out so many connections that sometimes my head hurts. But then I say a prayer of thanks that a word like *allusion* is not an excruciatingly boring term from a meaningless text. Allusions have become a part of our world; they have meaning. They are exciting, compelling, and worthy of more talking curriculum. They are, in other words, connected to the lives we live. And that leads and connects me to another thought, which is that for a very long time, I fought the idea of "doing subjects."

I remember the first time a neighbor child asked my children about their favorite subjects. My daughters were about six and eight years old, and they looked at their interrogator as if she were a Klingon. "What do you mean?" they asked.

I explained the whole school-and-subjects thing to them. I said that since they loved books of historical fiction, they could honestly say that two of their favorite subjects were reading and history. Or, because they loved to draw and paint, they could say art. Swimming and horseback riding were passions, so they could say P.E. I assured them it isn't actually necessary to break life down into subjects, though it can make chit-chat easier. And it can be helpful where the Dewey decimal system is concerned (and that, of course, led to another discussion). But, I made clear, they didn't have to start thinking in subjects.

When children are very young, we naturally avoid breaking up the world that way. Babies and toddlers force us to live integrated lives in which we balance the many things that they are learning, doing, and mastering. During their infancy, we would find the overspecialization of later education to be absurd. We would never tell our babies, "Now this week we will focus only on eating with a spoon. None of this pulling-up-and-trying-to-walk business, for heaven's sake. That's not what we're studying right now." And yet somehow, as they get older, we feel the need to fragment and specialize.

When my oldest daughter, Emily, was three years old, life was one enormous web of connections. Reading a book about ducks led to talking about baby ducks. That led to thinking about baby people, which in turn led to playing with our own little baby person, Lizzy. That, in turn, led to counting Lizzy's fingers and toes. Amidst satisfied giggles from Lizzy, Emily might then ask about how God made babies, and how did God make dirt, anyway? And did God have sisters? And speaking of dirt, could we go outside and play in some?

I could have said, "Hold your horses, one thing at a time! We can either talk about science [ducks and human reproduction], or math [counting those scrumptious little toes], or about theology [Does God have sisters?], or we can go do P.E. in the dirt. But we can't jumble it all up like that. One subject at a time, please!"

No. Emily didn't break the world into subjects and neither did I. Learning happened quickly and in a more integrated way when we allowed natural connections to influence our "studies." Most of us would probably agree that in many areas of our society specialization can and does lead to fragmentation. Parsing education into subjects, which are then studied in a vacuum apart from other subjects, can also lead to a fragmented understanding of both the subjects and the world around us.

One might argue that while it is fun and beneficial for a toddler to follow connections in such a haphazard way, as children grow, a certain amount of specialization is necessary. I agree. A *certain* amount is necessary. As children mature we can zoom in, focusing on particular interests in greater depth. But that increased degree of focus does not have to be at the exclusion of connecting those interests to the rest of life. My experience (and of course, that is all

I am finally talking about here) is that making connections and looking for the ways in which the "subjects" of life are interwoven paves the way to a greater understanding of both education and life. For example, when my kids and I recently read about Archimedes, were we covering history or math or science? The kids didn't really care what we called it. The reading was interesting. We were learning.

So our history studies are full of literature. Our literature marches through history. History is interlaced with science, and everything points to our Faith. When my kids read a book about World War II and we end up discussing Hitler, the problem of evil, hatred, the dignity of all human beings, racism, personal responsibility, and Christian duty, I can check off boxes labeled history, social studies, citizenship, reading comprehension, and religion, without ever purchasing a workbook specific to any of these things. I don't actually have such boxes to check off, mind you. I do, however, keep learning notes about everything we read, discuss, and study.

You get the point. Subjects are rarely neat and tidy, and life is an integrated whole. Again, for us school is life, life is school, and talking is most of our curriculum.

So far, I've discussed the way in which I make plans, only to see the plans lead us far beyond my intentions. But I must add that sometimes our connections grow not out of a deviation from the master plan but simply and spontaneously.

A while back, my daughters and I watched a video on YouTube of a dad singing his bedtime version of Pachelbel's *Canon in D*. The kids found the clip as funny and endearing as I did, and we listened to it several times. That prompted me to be sure they knew what was being parodied. I didn't call what followed music class, nor did I gather them for a quiz after amassing a number of facts. We just investigated together, and we talked.

First, we found several different versions of Pachelbel's *Canon in D* on YouTube. We watched everything from a professional video to some high-school kids performing in a basement. Then I found our Pachelbel CD and played that for them as well.

A couple of days later, while at the dentist for check-ups, I heard the piece playing over the office radio. Emily later remarked, "Mom! Did you hear Pachelbel's *Canon* while you were getting your teeth cleaned?"

The next night, as my husband sat in the living room grading English papers (as a high-school teacher, he does have to deal with subjects), he listened to a classical music radio station. Something floated sweetly through the air. I was combing my five-year-old's wet hair as she read *Winter Days in the Big Woods*. Kate suddenly looked up, and asked, "What is this?"

"You mean this music?" asked Tom.

I knew exactly what she was thinking. I had been thinking the same thing. The piece, some sort of chamber music, sounded familiar. I asked her, "What does it sound like to you?" She listened for a moment, and then said, "Pachelbel."

Tom and I agreed that it had the same sweet, layered sound, although we didn't know the name of the piece. It wasn't *Canon in D*, but it was something similar.

When our daughter left the room, Tom said of her observation, "I know nature plays a part, but nurture has an awful lot to do with it." I agree. Living in an atmosphere of inquisitiveness allows for natural learning—for making connections. Paying attention to the tiny details that surround us, taking time to investigate, wandering down unexpected, untrodden paths, listening to what captivates my children, or sharing my own enthusiasm for an idea—all of these things allow for spontaneous and flexible learning that makes an impression on our children and stays with them.

Charlotte Mason, in her book *Philosophy of Education*, said that education is "an atmosphere, a discipline, a life" (94). I hope this is true in our home. It is certainly what I aim for. I can't say that every night sees our living room awash in an atmosphere of calm or sophisticated culture. It doesn't. Some nights, the kids seem anything but cultured, I'm tired and crabby, and we all have trouble acting civilized. Other nights we laugh at Alton Brown and Food Network silliness, with nary a great composer in sight—though I could do another entire chapter on the Food Network Curriculum. But all of this is okay. I don't measure education one day at a time; I look at the bigger picture. I measure both educational progress and happiness on a larger scale: What kind of week did we have? What kind of month? Or autumn? What kind of year? What kind of *life* are we living?

What the unschooling equation ultimately means to this Planning Unschooler is that we are free of the institutional model of school, a model which dictates a classroom, predetermined curricula for particular ages, and school hours carved in stone. We are free to be everywhere in our education. We can "do school" at 11 P.M. if that is when we're into one of the best conversations we've ever had. We are free to blend planned studies and Mom-initiated topics with unstructured, child-driven projects, books, ideas, and discussions.

It's all up to us, because we are the architects. We have built an un-classroom, we keep un-hours, and we have un-preconceived notions. My grand catalog-inspired plans always develop and unfold, and just as surely, portions of them fall by the wayside. But the main thing I plan for every year happens without fail: we talk and we learn. And that answer to the unschooling equation gets an A in our classroom. Which, incidentally, is in the kitchen today.

CHAPTER THIRTEEN

Faith's Family: My Love-Hate Relationship with Unschooling

Faith Roberts attended Mount St. Mary's College in Emmitsburg, and she went on to receive her law degree from the University of Maryland Law School. Although she passed three bar exams, she has never actually practiced law; she finds homeschooling much more fun. Her husband was a stand-up comic for a year after college but hated hanging out in bars, so he ended up in law school as well. The Roberts and their five children (aged nine to twenty) make their home in Virginia, where they have been homeschooling for fourteen years. Their oldest daughter is a Sophomore at the University of Dallas, on the Dean's List and about to spend a semester in Rome. Their oldest son was just accepted to Berklee College of Music. Faith writes about her family and unschooling on the blog Strewing.

Do small things with great love.

—Mother Teresa

Unschooling happens all the time. It is nothing more than natural learning, that is, the taking in of information and processing it. As far as I can tell, this kind of learning is practically unavoidable. A baby learns in utero when he becomes familiar with the sound of his mother's heartbeat and his mother's voice, when he discovers how to suck his thumb and that kicking and stretching and doing somersaults is fun. A newborn baby is a little sponge soaking up even more: how to breathe, cry, suckle, and how to recognize his mother's face. And of course children learn language at an amazing speed.

As I see it, the next level of learning is not just taking in and responding to what is around us, but pursuing a depth of knowledge about things that spark an interest. This is a natural process too. Those who have a passion or hobby are basically unschooling themselves, and usually we have more than one enthusiasm going at a time.

Illustrations are all around us. My fifteen-year-old son got interested in guitar a year ago and begged for lessons. We had an old acoustic guitar hanging around the house already, we agreed to pay for lessons, and he took off. In addition to taking lessons, he has been studying theory on his own and learning about many types of music. He knows about guitar players from B. B. King to Eric Clapton, but his fascination with music hasn't stopped with rock and roll. The other day I caught him listening to Faure's *Requiem*; he said he wanted to expand his horizons. He loved it. He has started his own band and has begun writing his own songs. He is filled with an intense love for music, so it is a joy to watch him work hard and immerse himself in something he obviously has a talent for. The satisfaction of delving intensely into something that gives back so much pleasure is truly a beautiful gift.

From my own experience and from witnessing how my children explore the world around them, I have come to believe unschooling, or natural learning, is a fact of life. So if I am sold on unschooling, why am I of two minds about it? Why do I have a love-hate relationship with this style of homeschooling, and why can't I ever be a pure unschooler (at least not for very long)?

To answer these questions, I need to tell my homeschooling story from the beginning. This son that I have mentioned was the child that got us started; he was different from the get-go, always marching to his own drumbeat. I had him in the same sweet, private, preschool program my older daughter had so enjoyed and thrived in, but he was miserable. He was in his own separate universe while all the other kids were orbiting together on the other side of the room. I was in a quandary the following summer: Should we send him to kindergarten at the school where he was currently miserable, or should we send him to the public school to be miserable there?

While mulling over this no-win situation, our family went on a long weekend visit to a horse farm down in Charlottesville, Virginia. We stayed in a little cabin on the farm; the kids got to ride horses and swim in the pool, and we also did lots of sightseeing around the area. Or, I should clarify, my husband did all this with the kids. I read. The woman who owned the farm was a homeschooler. Not only was she a homeschooler, she was an unschooler. She had stocked the cabin bookshelves with books by Nancy Wallace and John Holt, and that is what I read for our three-day weekend, pretty much ignoring the rest of the family. By the end of that weekend, I was convinced that I wanted to homeschool. And scared to death, I might add. It was a powerful conversion experience for me, and I attribute it to the work of the Holy Spirit.

My husband agreed to a probationary year. This concession took some doing, as he thought homeschoolers were the type of people who stockpiled weapons and lived in bunkers in South Dakota. That fall we got our son diagnosed by a neuropsychologist who labeled him ADHD/dyslexic. Let me mention that I've had problems with this label for years, but the truth was that this child really didn't take in information in the usual way. We saw him left in the dust as other children raced ahead picking up various skills that they seemed to grasp fairly naturally. He simply didn't and couldn't.

For my part, I was exploring many aspects of homeschooling, not only unschooling. Early on I read *A Charlotte Mason Companion* by Karen Andreola, and I'd also read *The Lost Tools of Learning* by Dorothy L. Sayers along with Laura Berquist's *Designing Your Own Classical Curriculum*.

I loved the idea of unschooling and the gentleness of Karen Andreola's take on Charlotte Mason. Both these approaches to homeschooling seemed to present an idyllic way of learning and growing. We already did lots of things that were educational with our kids. I had read aloud to them since they were in the womb, practically; we watched our fair share of educational TV, from which we all learned a great deal (I am especially thankful to Bill Nye for explaining science to me after those endless classes in school failed to do the trick). We went on walks and nature hikes and field trips, and we spent time doing arts and crafts. We found the world of early childhood was easily filled with educational experiences.

At the same time, I was attracted to classical education. I had received an extremely favorable impression of it from my father. My mother was always proud of my father's Jesuit education. I had merely considered him a super smart guy, especially handy to have around when you were trying to read a Latin inscription on the front of some stately building. Now I began to appreciate the advantages and breadth of his schooling.

Consequently, the thought of giving my children (and myself in the bargain) a classical education was thrilling. To plumb the depths of the great works and thought of Western Civilization seemed like a heady challenge, to be conversant in the writings of Aristotle and Aquinas seemed so noble, broadening and grounding at the same time. To partake of that clarity of thought, that wide scope of understanding, that depth of wisdom, well, it seemed to me—and still seems—to be a wonderful way to pass one's time while here on earth. Reality, however, took me down from these noble aspirations. I was busy having babies and waiting for my older children to acquire the skill of reading. And this is where I first began to run into trouble with unschooling.

When I began to realize that my children were not going to start magically reading on their own at the age of four simply because I read out loud to them frequently, I had to readjust my expectations a little. I myself had learned to read before I started kindergarten. My older sister and I had loved playing school. There were a lot of beginning readers lying around the house, and we used these in our pretend school. My nine-year-old sister taught me the letter sounds and helped me piece together the sounds into words, and I took off reading from there. Obviously my very bright children would do the same, right? It didn't happen.

The long and short of it is that through our family's experiences, I have come to believe that there actually are such things as genuine learning disabilities. That may be an unfortunate term for the phenomena, but I don't think that the learning of certain skills, such as reading, comes naturally to everyone. A significant number of people need help in acquiring these skills, and my children were among them.

Not surprisingly, our struggle with reading, with simply becoming literate, made me rethink how I wanted to homeschool my kids. While I enjoyed many aspects of unschooling, there were ways it didn't seem to be enough for us. On the one hand, my oldest three children always did fine with unschooling math; they were quite natural learners in that regard. But on the other hand, in addition to our difficulties trying to unschool reading, I didn't care for the unstructured, scattered way in which our unschooling days took shape. And here I must confess that I am a contradiction. I naturally resist structure, yet without it, I fall apart. My kids reflected this trait as well.

When our days were unstructured, my children (one of them in particular) would go into a free-fall emotionally. When our days were structured my children tended to behave better, seeming more content and sociable. In this particular area, I needed more guidance than the unschooling philosophy provided, yet I felt guilty every time I wanted to impose order from above.

I can see now that there were reasons for this guilt beyond what unschooling did or did not supply. First, I was going through a struggle in understanding how to discipline my children. I wanted to be sweet and positive and joyful in my parenting, but too often I was cranky and impatient. In retrospect I see that I didn't yet know myself well enough to understand that I am really an introvert. I needed time by myself to recharge, yet like many Catholic mothers, I was always surrounded by children. They were making demands, requiring me to come to a hundred little decisions a day, and providing more than a hundred distractions a day as well. Parenting is very wearing, emotionally and physically. Now don't get me wrong—I love being a parent. I love that God has blessed us with five children, but I must be honest and say that parenting tests the mettle of one's character more than most other life situations.

And meanwhile, what happened with our homeschooling? Unschooling, although helpful in some areas, was not working for us in others. So I did what any self-respecting Catholic homeschooling mother would do: I decided to go classical.

I read *The Well-Trained Mind.* Actually, I reread it. The first time I read it, I hated it. Wouldn't you know that it too presented the same bit about how teaching kids to read is easy? The second time through, however, I let that go and used the rest to help me determine a course for our academic life. My oldest daughter enrolled in a Latin class for homeschooled middle schoolers, we started reading history in a systematic way, and we began working from math books more consistently. I spent a great deal of time planning and replanning, trying to fit all these wonderful studies into a rich classical education.

I got into a pattern. I'd start off gung-ho in the fall with all this fabulous new curricula. For me, planning and curricula buying is a heavenly occupation. By the time Christmas rolled around, I'd be completely burned out. I'd spend the next couple of months limping along. I'd cut back drastically to just read-alouds and a couple of math or spelling/writing sessions a week. Then Lent would arrive and that spirit of sacrifice and self-control would infect my attitude toward schooling. A further incentive to serious study would arise as we faced end-of-the-year standardized testing, which we do to meet our state's homeschooling statutes.

"Well," I'd say, "I really should prepare the children for these tests . . . to be fair to them." So in the spring I'd get back into the swing of things and be a bit more structured again.

We did this through my oldest daughter's ninth grade year, but that year I burned out terribly. I think it was the strain of doing high school for the first time, dealing with growing resistance from my children, and still struggling to get younger kids reading. And of course life and death didn't slow down for a minute. My mother had passed away four years into our homeschooling journey. My father had severe health problems and passed away four years later. I had health issues. Every year there was something that got in the way of our pure, unadulterated pursuit of classical education. I felt like I was running in sand, working so hard and never getting anywhere.

And I saw that my kids had lost all love of learning. They were tired of being treated like empty buckets to be filled. They wanted to be left alone. When they did have free moments during our structured phases, mostly they wanted to pursue totally mindless activities. Oddly, when I was in my annual winter slump and wasn't imposing on them with my usual level of intensity, I noticed they always took off with something interesting, inspired by read-aloud or a movie, a conversation, a visit, a friend's new-found interest, or an outside activity.

So I returned to unschooling. It had the answers to these problems, even if it didn't have absolutely everything I needed. Now, whenever I see what we do as unschooling, the vision is colored by the additional glow of some other educational philosophy. I have studied the many influences prominent in homeschooling, and what else can I say? In all honesty, I must add that I am easily bored! My solution is to freely incorporate many different approaches, depending on what appeals to us and works for us at the time. Charlotte Mason, unit studies, Montessori, and Waldorf have all been part of our homeschool landscape. None of them takes root very deeply, but they all definitely inspire and energize me.

Sometimes I feel like a ping-pong ball, going back and forth between two extremes. Lately I have been heavily influenced by *The Latin Centered Curriculum*. After mainly unschooling again for a year and half, once more I found myself floundering. We had gone into our free-fall of being too unstructured, and we were ready to recover some focus. *The Latin Centered Curriculum* concentrates on the basics of Latin and Greek, math, and literacy. The rest to be learned comes through the reading of certain seminal books on the different subjects. This leaves lots of room for independent reading, nature walks, fun outside classes, and the exploration of interests and passions. In other words, it blends our favorite aspects of both unschooling and classical learning.

I believe natural learning is very much like breathing; it happens unconsciously and all the time. It is a part of living and a part of being human, but there are some things that my family prefers to study in a more formal way. What works best for us is balancing formal study times with our informal learning, and allowing the children to have as much say as possible regarding how we pursue it all. I like to make it enjoyable for them, with plenty of interaction in every type of learning. For my family, a hybrid of classical and unschooling seems to work best.

It is hard for me to believe that twelve years have passed since we began our homeschooling journey. As I look back, I see that all along we have been searching for equilibrium. When one is trying to balance, it requires a constant shifting in order to stay upright, and that is what I feel defines our homeschooling style. Oftentimes I have felt unstable, wishing I could just choose one method and stick to it. But that doesn't seem to give us stability either, for then we lean too far to one side and fall. Consequently, I've come to terms with our ever-changing combinations, and look forward to continuing my family's balancing act as we learn, love, and serve the Lord together.

CHAPTER FOURTEEN

Melissa's Family: Tidal Homeschooling

Melissa Wiley and her husband are the parents of six children ranging in age from a toddler to a fifteen-year-old; their family lives in Southern California. Melissa has coined the phrase Tidal Learning *to describe her family's homeschooling style. She is the author of* The Martha Years *and* The Charlotte Years *series (historical novels for children, based on the lives of Laura Ingalls Wilder's great grandmother and grandmother). Melissa writes regularly about books and family life at her blog,* Here in the Bonny Glen.

> *Life should be all living, and not merely a tedious passing of time; not all doing or all feeling or all thinking—the strain would be too great—but, all living; that is to say, we should be in touch wherever we go, whatever we hear, whatever we see, with some manner of vital interest . . . The question is not—how much does the youth know when he has finished his education—but how much does he care?*
>
> —Charlotte Mason, *School Education*

People often ask me what kind of homeschoolers we are: Classical? Charlotte Mason? Eclectic? Delight-directed? Unschoolers? What they want to know is: How does learning happen in my home? Am I in charge, or do I let the kids lead the way? And what about math?

Over the years I have written with enthusiasm about the Charlotte Mason method (which is highly structured) and unschooling (which is not). These educational philosophies seem to have become intertwined in my home, so that *what we do*—read great books, study nature, dive deeply into history, immerse ourselves in picture study and composer study—is highly influenced by Charlotte Mason and her modern counterparts, and *how we do it*—through strewing and conversation and leisurely, child-led exploration—is influenced by the writings of John Holt, Sandra Dodd, and other advocates of unschooling. But I couldn't say we are "real CMers" because I don't carry out Miss Mason's recommendations in anything like the structured manner she prescribed; on the other hand, I do too much behind-the-scenes nudging for us to be considered radical unschoolers.

The truth is, I couldn't find any label that completely fit my family, so I made up my own. I call us "tidal learners" because the ways in which we approach education change with the tide. This doesn't mean that we're flighty or inconsistent, changing direction haphazardly. We aren't Fiddler Crab Homeschoolers. What I mean is that there is a rhythm to the way learning happens here; there are upbeats and downbeats; there is an ebb and flow.

We have high tide times when I charter a boat and we set sail with purpose and direction, deliberately casting our net for a particular type of fish. On these excursions I am often the captain; I have charted the course. But the children are eager crew members because they know I value their contributions. And I also provide generous rations. No stale or moldy bread on this ship: no dull textbooks, no dry workbooks. My sailors sink their teeth into fresh, hearty bread slathered with rich butter and tart-sweet jam. Well fed and proud of their work, my little crew exhilarates in the voyage. Every journey is an adventure.

And we have low tide times when we amble along the shore, peering into tide pools and digging in the sand, or just relaxing under a beach umbrella. The children wander off in directions of their own choosing; they dig and poke and ponder. One of them may crouch over a rock pool and stay there for days, studying, watching. Another will run headlong into the waves, thrilling to the pull on her legs, splashing, leaping, diving under and emerging triumphantly farther out. Or a child might prefer to stay close by my side, drawing stick pictures in the sand or building a castle. All of these things may be happening at once. Sometimes it looks as though nothing is happening; there's just an array of bodies on beach towels. But oh, the nourishment there is in a time of quiet reflection while the soul soaks up the sunlight!

Our family enjoys both kinds of learning—the heady adventure of the well-planned fishing trip, with a goal and a destination in mind, and the mellower joys of undirected discovery during weeks at the metaphorical beach. Around here, the low tide times happen much more frequently than the high tide times, and often I find that the children catch more fish, so to speak, when the tide is out. Beachcombing reveals many treasures. But they do enjoy their fishing-boat excursions with Cap'n Mom. I believe joy is the key, the element we breathe whether the tide is in or out. It's the wind that propels our ship, the tangy breeze that cools and refreshes us on the beach.

"So what exactly do you do all day?" is a question I'm repeatedly asked; that is, what does the metaphor look like in real, everyday life? Since every day is different, it's easiest to answer that question with snapshots and specifics. Right now, this month, we are in high tide. We spend our mornings on the boat, so to speak, studying Latin and German; we are enjoying a Tennyson poem every day; we're reading a book of American history together as well as the engaging children's classic *My Side of the Mountain*. My thirteen-year-old is working her way through a chemistry course, of her own volition. My ten-year-old is writing a story (I haven't been allowed to see it yet), and my seven-year-old has requested drawing lessons, so we are working together on the exercises in *Drawing with Kids*.

We very often get into a high tide groove in the fall. Often I'll find that the tide begins to go out sometime around mid-November, just in time for Advent. This year we are expecting a baby around Epiphany, so I won't be at all surprised if low tide lasts until spring.

During low tide, we maintain the most basic rhythms of our days: mealtimes, chore times, prayer times. But the rest of the day is wide open. I don't direct anyone to pull out a Latin book (though a child may wind up pulling it out on her own) or to "do math." I might suggest someone take a look at a book I think she'll like, but she isn't under any obligation to read it.

One important point is that even in our most casual low tide times, the metaphorical beach my children are exploring is a beach I myself have strewn with treasures in advance. *Strewing* is a term coined by radical unschooling guru Sandra Dodd, and it means leaving interesting and educational materials—books, games, puzzles, supplies—in the path of a child. If I notice a child is enjoying a book on Greek myths, I might pull a few other books off the shelf and leave them on an end table where the child will find them, or send her the link to an interesting website, or pop an audio version of *The Odyssey* into the minivan's CD player.

Another way of strewing is to get immersed in an activity or subject myself. Rather than announce to the children, "Now it's time to work on your nature notebooks," I might sit down at the table with my own nature journal and some Prismacolor pencils. Before you can say "California poppy," I'm likely to have been joined by one or more children asking if they can draw in their journals too.

Strewing is something unschooling parents talk a great deal about. I believe it is the same thing Charlotte Mason meant when she said, "Education is a life. That life is sustained on ideas . . . . We must sustain a child's inner life with ideas as we sustain his body with food" (*Parents and Children*, 39). She was urging parents and teachers to provide hearty feasts of "living" books and firsthand encounters with the natural world. Of course, Miss Mason recommended regular and orderly mealtimes, while an unschooler would probably say that the human mind thrives best when allowed to graze. But in both cases, we see a committed, thoughtful parent doing the shopping and preparing the food. I am doing just as much preparation (to jump metaphors again) during our low tide times as I am during high tide. Whether I am piloting the boat on a fishing trip—as I am doing now with our studies of German and Latin—or hiding bits of sea glass in the sand for a wandering child to discover (or not), my role is the one Charlotte Mason called "guide, philosopher, and friend" (*Towards a Philosophy of Education*, 32).

Some radical unschoolers would not consider my family's high tide times to be compatible with unschooling philosophy. To be honest, I don't trouble myself overmuch about the philosophy. I do what works, and what makes sense. As a Catholic, I often find that I am approaching education—and life, for that matter—from an angle quite different from that of secular unschoolers.

Catholicism accepts and indeed embraces certain limits (that which we may not do) and obligations (that which we must do). In my experience, all parents, including the most radical unschoolers, impose some kind of limits and expectations upon their children. A radical secular unschooler might not require chores, might not make a child practice piano, but will almost always hold a child to certain standards of behavior in one way or another. For example, the parent may draw a rather firm line regarding how it is okay or not okay to treat other people. The parent may seem extremely hands-off compared to other parents, perhaps allowing the child to eat and sleep on his own schedule rather than according to a family routine, or allowing unlimited video game time. But finally the most relaxed radical unschooling parent is likely to consider certain things nonnegotiable: It is never okay to bully another person, take what does not belong to you, and so forth.

As a Catholic mother, I may have more nonnegotiables than a secular unschooling mother would. For my children, pitching in with family chores is a nonnegotiable. So is attending Mass with the family every Sunday. By the same logic, there are certain elements of my children's education which I feel are important enough to direct to a degree which might not seem unschoolish to some unschoolers.

Of course, *unschooling* is a word notoriously hard to define. If your definition involves allowing children complete freedom to choose what and how and when to learn (albeit with a great deal of dialogue with parents, and an environment richly strewn with resources), then I am unschoolish but not a pure unschooler.

I am on board with most of the elements of that definition. Parental connection and involvement leading to lively discussion? Check. Allowing children a role in the selection of topics or skills to explore? Check. Taking into account the individual learning style, temperament, and changing interests of each child? Check. Environment richly strewn with educational resources? Check plus plus.

The only place I depart from that definition, really, is in the word *complete*. I allow a great deal of freedom when it comes to learning, but complete freedom? No, I can't say that applies to us. As I said, I do steer the ship for certain subjects and seasons. We may spend most of the year in low tide, but we do have our high tide times.

Where I connect with unschooling is in the understanding that people of all ages learn best when they *want* to learn, are interested in the subject, and feel joy in the process, and that standard classroom educational methods are not necessarily, or even usually, the best ways to learn. Children have such an eager appetite for knowledge (it is, as Charlotte Mason says, the food their minds are made to live on) that it is not, in my opinion, at all necessary to turn the experience of gaining knowledge into a drudgery, conflict, or carrot-and-stick experience.

Where I depart from unschooling is in my understanding that adults have a wider perspective than children, are (it is to be hoped) wiser than children, and that this is quite natural and proper. And just as my parental wisdom and experience direct me to provide a nutritious diet for my children, so do they direct me to provide a rich and nourishing menu of ideas and learning experiences for their growing minds.

When I think about knowledge, I see that everything I can think of falls into one of two categories: content or skills. By *content* I mean facts, ideas, principles, stories. History, literature, much of science—all content knowledge which can be learned quite effortlessly, naturally, one might even say accidentally, the way people absorb information about subjects in which they are interested.

Skill knowledge generally requires a degree of concentrated effort, practice, step-by-step progress. For many people, arithmetic falls into the skill knowledge category; most of us have to learn it on purpose, so to speak. We progress through steps, mastering each step in turn.

Playing a musical instrument, speaking a foreign language, learning to draw—these are other skills which most (but certainly not all) people have to learn on purpose, requiring practice and diligence in order to achieve mastery. Learning to read may fall into this category for many people, but I really cannot speak to that since I have now had four children learn to read quite accidentally.

In any case, that's how I see it. Because there are certain skills I believe are exceedingly useful to possess, those are the subjects I am inclined to direct during our high tide times if I perceive that *accidental* learning is not taking place.

Thus far, however, my experience has been that almost all of the skills I think important enough to require are things the children are keenly interested in anyway. They want to learn to play piano and to draw well; they want to be able to calculate how much money they must save up in order to buy a book or toy they've set their hearts on. Usually my role is to gently (and once in a while, firmly) nudge them along when the first flare of enthusiasm for a pursuit wears out. And yes, I "make" them practice piano, but that really just means reminding them to sit down on the bench. From there, their own interest takes over.

My ten-year-old's enthusiasm for Latin ebbs and flows, but there again my nudging is usually only a matter of getting her over the hump. Often she will grumble about having to begin, but then she'll grumble again when I say it is time to do something else. I think this really has more to do with her innate resistance to change than a reluctance toward the subject. Transitions of any kind are difficult for this child.

As a Charlotte Mason-inspired mother with a strong unschooling bent, I see one of my primary roles as that of careful observer. I have observed what very real delight my children take in mastering a new piece of music or in figuring out the meaning of an unfamiliar word because they recognize its Latin root. I have seen how enthusiastically they've embraced books which seemed, perhaps, a trifle dry at first glance, but which improved in their estimation after I read a few chapters aloud. These experiences and countless others like them are why I don't see our high tide times as incompatible with the label "unschooling." It would be fair to say that high tide is another kind of strewing.

However you define it or describe it, the reality that we have enjoyed for a decade now is one of rich, lively, joyful learning experiences. Whether I am piloting my young sailors out of the harbor on a more formal fishing expedition or watching them build sandcastles and hunt for pearls in oysters, what I see are eager and knowledge-hungry children exploring the world with great relish. They are enjoying one another's company, connecting with people and events and ideas, and expressing awe and wonder over the magnificence of God's creation. Come squall or smooth sailing, they are viewing all of life as a grand adventure.

CHAPTER FIFTEEN

Willa's Family: Holding the Center

Willa Ryan and her husband are the parents of seven children, now aged eight to twenty-four. The family lives in the mountains of central California; they have been homeschooling for seventeen years. Alongside unschooling, Willa's main educational approach is the classical method. She writes regularly on her blog Quotidian Moments *and moderates the Catholic Classical Education e-list.*

> *How much more profitable for the independent mind, after the mere rudiments of education, to range through a library at random, taking down books as they meet him, and pursuing the trains of thought which his mother wit suggests! How much healthier to wander into the fields, and there with the exiled Prince to find "tongues in the trees, books in the running brooks!"*
>
> —Blessed John Henry Cardinal Newman
> *Idea of a University*

Unschooling gave me the courage and inspiration to start homeschooling in the first place. And even now it seems like the heart of what we do in our homeschool, though you may find us sitting down at regular intervals with a checklist and a math or Latin text. Unschooling is the goal for us, because my ideal is for my children to have what, according to George Weigel, Pope John Paul II called "freedom for excellence" ("A Better Concept of Freedom"). I want them to choose to learn, and to participate in what is good, true, and beautiful without making a distinction between learning and everything else in life.

Of course, such ideals aren't unique to unschoolers, and in fact, I have had trouble discerning whether what we do in any given day is unschooling or not. Is it unschooling when I sit down with my twelve-year-old to read to him from books that I cherish, but that he might not pick up on his own? Can you still call yourself an unschooler if you assign a saint's biography for daily reading? What if then, as recently happened, the child loves the book, finishes it in a week, and devours two more saints' books in the next two days? What about a high schooler who designs her own course of study which turns out to be a fairly rigorous college prep course? What she's doing looks a lot like formal school, yet she works entirely self-propelled, receiving only support and conversation from mom. Is that unschooling, or is it something else? When I know my nine-year-old would rather be playing with Hot Wheels, but I sit down with him for a reading lesson because I believe that reading will open a treasure chest to him, am I going against the ethos of unschooling?

I struggled for a long time trying to discern the answer. In different seasons of our lives we have gone from classical to Charlotte Mason, then to what looked more like unschooling, that is, simply living richly, talking and playing and reading, and investigating what caught our attention. Over time I came to realize that all these approaches were similar in several ways under the surface, and some of the tension I felt trying to balance my ideals with the often not-so-pretty details of daily life began to dissipate. I came to recognize that real learning is a living thing. It will look different from family to family, from child to child, from season to season.

Unschooling is a concept oriented to freedom and individuality, and thus I should not be concerned with trying to measure up to someone else's homeschooling or unschooling endeavor. I only need to do what I am called to do, using the principles which I hold true. Unschooling helps me examine what I do, which enables me to stay close to the center of things and not be distracted by unnecessary requirements. I could easily become a Martha of homeschooling, focused on the trivial tasks. Unschooling reminds me of Mary's truth that there is a center, still and quiet, and my necessary task is to sit close and listen.

Because of these things, I see unschooling as the center or core of my homeschooling, even though the outside forms it takes may look different during different times of our lives. I could say that family relationships are at the core of our homeschooling, and it would be close to saying the same thing. Let me tell you a little about our life, and you can see what I mean.

We started homeschooling seventeen years ago, when my eldest had finished second grade in the parish school of a university town. At that time we also had a child in kindergarten, and two who weren't yet of school age. Now we have seven children, and we live in a log home in the Sierra Mountains, with towering trees around us. If you came inside our home, you would probably notice the high ceilings (sometimes decorated with cobwebs), the large hearth with a wood stove and an icon of Our Lady on the mantel, the computers of various degrees of advancement, the music center upstairs, and the books. Books are everywhere.

At its fullest, the house contained nine family members: seven children, and their father and mother. Now the oldest child has graduated from a Catholic liberal arts college and is working as a computer game designer. Two of his siblings are in college; the younger of these two, our only girl, is a sophomore at the Catholic college her brother attended. The four youngest range in age from eight to seventeen years old.

My husband works at home as a freelance computer game designer. His professional situation has provided an ongoing example of work integrated with family life, as well as giving his growing boys an opportunity to apprentice in a trade. And what about the mother? I am a convert, and every day I wake up feeling grateful to have the treasury of Church literature and liturgy available to me. It is the air that I breathe, and the environment around me, just as the clear mountain air and towering pines, sequoias, and cedars around us are integral parts of our home's environment.

Around the time we started homeschooling, I had only recently been confirmed in the Catholic Faith. In my mind, learning was divided into two categories: the often painful, stressful information-piling mode of the schools I had attended, and the things I read and did on my own time, whenever I could catch a few spare moments. The first kind of learning seemed to leave no real tracks on my personality, except the fear and aversion they impressed; the second kind was a delight. When my husband asked me about homeschooling our children, I pictured the first kind of schooling (at home), and I couldn't imagine inflicting it on my kids.

Somehow I found the homeschooling section of our library and started to read. Providentially, the university town library was stocked with the books of John Holt, Raymond and Dorothy Moore, and Nancy Wallace. These early homeschooling pioneers wrote in the days when keeping your children out of school often meant suspicion and intervention from the school system and could result in court appearances. These books, and Holt's *Growing Without Schooling* grassroots newsletter, were compelling to me because they spoke to themes I was beginning to consciously understand: the importance of a strong family and its key role in the raising of children; the right of parents to bring their children up in a unique, nonstandardized manner; and the amazing ability of children to learn what they need to know in a supportive, loving environment.

When the term *unschooling* was coined, it was a reaction against what schools had become. Until I looked into the matter closely, I had never thought about it this way because I took schools for granted, disliked or not, as necessary institutions. But the conventional school of our day is very different from the schoolhouses of previous generations. This is a subject too big to go into here, but suffice it to say that once I began reading about the background of our American educational system, I realized that what I had disliked and resisted in my school years was this form of modern schooling. It was planned and programmed to be scientifically efficient using a factory-type model.

I do not mean to say that all schools before this century were wonderful places; Charles Dickens and Charlotte Bronte are two of the authors who have testified in literary form to the contrary. I would not even say that schools today are all harmful, because I've known many schools and, particularly, many teachers who did wonderful things to educate children. But the reading I did as I began to think about homeschooling put unschooling into a historical context.

The original unschoolers were not rejecting learning or excellence; rather, they were seeking these prizes. They were rejecting instead the tyranny of a specific kind of government control, which had taken away the parents' right and duty to choose the form of education they thought best for their children. The first homeschools were in some ways parallel to the Irish hedge schools, which operated literally under cover after the British occupants had taken away the Irish people's schools, or like the Polish cultural clubs that Karol Wojtyla and his friends operated during the days of Nazi and Soviet occupation in Poland. The early homeschoolers were subversive too, but in a similarly positive and necessary way, and the chronicles of their children's learning inspired me.

As I was reading these stories of adventure and courage and freedom, I was also privileged to have a weekly holy hour at our church's Perpetual Adoration chapel. The graces I received were immense. One was my realization that the center of reality is not the active surface, not the parish bulletin, the coffee and donuts after Mass, nor the community outreach, as good and holy as these things are. The center, the heart of the Church—of everything, indeed—is the silent Presence, hidden in the chapel, lit only by a dim candle.

In his poem "The Second Coming," Yeats wrote, "Things fall apart/the center does not hold," but indeed, the true center will hold. As members of the Mystical Body, we are intimately connected to the center, and as the Jesuit Father John Hardon has explained, we Catholic families have a major part in holding this center of things (Mirus, "The Blueprint for Heroic Family Life"). In many ways, though society may marginalize us, we *are* the center. I saw this truth particularly embodied in the practice of unschooling, and yet, paradoxically, it is in unschooling that we can also feel rather on the edge of things.

The 1996 Education Act of the United Kingdom calls homeschooling "Education Otherwise," and so when I'm feeling on the outer margin, I often say to myself that we are doing it "otherwise." In a healthy biosphere there is usually an outer edge, and this outer edge often possesses the hardiness and diversity that benefits the biosphere as a whole. In other words, the outside, the sign of contradiction, is often the salt that preserves the main body. You might say that holding the center does not always require one to stand at the center.

How, then, have I tried to hold the center to the best of my ability? By focusing on the individuality of the children, amid the changing circumstances of our lives. Sometimes, the result has clearly been unschooling.

For example, when we first moved to our log home here in the California mountains, the house was still being finished around us, and we decided to make the most of our situation. The kids went outside and explored their fresh environment; they used measuring devices to measure things; they played with some of their toys that had been in storage for a year; they wrote stories, and later, my husband read them the entire Lord of the Rings trilogy by the light of the fire in our new wood stove. Our curriculum was one of change and growth, but the center still held in the family closeness of the hearth and the good book.

Another occasion for simply holding the center came nine years ago when my sixth child was born. Almost immediately he had to be transferred to a university hospital over two hundred miles away, where he stayed for several months before and after his liver transplant. To be with him, we moved temporarily to the city and stayed in a small apartment; we wanted him to have his family around him as much as possible. During this time, while we were mostly preoccupied with medical ups and downs, our formal schooling shrunk to a simple reading and discussion time at night when I came home from the hospital. Much of our evening time was spent playing, talking, or just cuddling, often in front of a TV, since I was too exhausted to do much more. Our family life and our Faith were the center that held even when everything else was in flux.

Then again at other periods, such as the start of a school year, we have been quite structured. During more ordinary seasons in our life, I usually plan carefully and we start off the autumn in a somewhat formal mode. By Advent we have often gone in directions that have taken us rather far from the original plans. I used to feel guilty about spending all that time planning and then failing to follow through. But I have come to realize that this is a natural pattern for us and makes sense in several ways. When December comes we are usually in a basic household routine, and it is nice to be able to spend the next few cold months going on different learning tangents and reading lots of good books. We enjoy trying to do some of the crafts and liturgical activities that are so rich during these months of the year—although we are never very successful!

When Lent arrives there is time enough to begin reevaluating, taking stock of where we are and where we need to be by June, prepping for spring tests and evaluations. The weather is getting nicer, and we start heading out to partake of nature for a larger part of the day. In this season we get involved in more outside-the-home activities, such as spring sports. Then comes summer, the time to do family things. We go on trips and sometimes receive visitors, and have the opportunity to reorganize the house or do other extended projects that we have put off. And yet, while the outside details shift throughout the year, the center of literature, conversation, and nature, all in the context of our Faith and family relationships, holds firm.

Thinking in terms of patterns and rhythms, rather than merely plodding through school books, is an unschooling approach that has helped my understanding of what we are about. I think I first read about it in *Homeschooling for Excellence* by David and Micki Colfax. Their boys worked hard homesteading all spring, summer, and fall, and then spent the winter studying by lamplight, since they had no electricity. The boys ended up going to Ivy League colleges. Their way of life is reminiscent of that of another generation, when the school year was much shorter than it is now. Academic progress doesn't require hitting the schoolbooks for nine months out of every twelve, and we too have enjoyed letting a natural rhythm orchestrate our year.

Although we have now found the seasonal patterns that work for our family, over the years we have had our struggles with the problem that John Holt titled "What do I do Monday?" For a family attracted to unschooling, what replaces the conventional 9 A.M. to 3 P.M. day and the textbook/answer key way of schooling? Unschoolers sometimes say, "You just start living." Sound advice, but in my experience it has been difficult to figure out what such a life ought to look like. I have run into the temptation to stop doing with my children anything that might remotely be construed as schoolish, even things we all normally enjoy. An ironic obstacle, because it imitates the mistake of traditional school, dividing learning and normal life into two separate compartments. I used to fall into this trap regularly, and the only answer I could think of when it got too frustrating was to go back to a structured method. This in turn seemed to lead us to burnout and more frustration, because we were trying to do things in a way that did not suit our family. I love images, and I have resolved this dilemma by thinking about roots and seeds.

First, the image of roots. We live in an area of California where the trees tower way above us, but what allows them to grow to great heights is the understructure of roots, which are hidden from our sight. In a similar way, most of what kids learn academically is grounded on what they have acquired informally, on the mostly hidden understructure of their relationships with their family and with the world around them.

There are many familiar examples of this grounding. For instance, a baby gets his first concepts of matter and motion—physics—by manipulating objects in his environment. He pushes, pulls, drops, tugs, handles, and by the time he is a few years old he can pretty much predict (though not in words, necessarily) what will happen to a given object in given circumstances. He learns to talk in much the same way, by collecting assorted kinds of verbal information and finally trying to reproduce it. Again, most children when they learn to read have already had a rich literacy background of enjoying read-aloud stories, seeing words on a page, perhaps scribbling "stories" of their own. Math concepts too are grounded in a similar context of experience with seeing numbers, counting objects, and observing patterns. Even most character and behavior formation is only successful in an environment where there is a consistent example. And finally, fundamentally all learning is grounded on attachment. A loving relationship with parents is the root system upon which any further character and intellectual efforts are built.

When the child has enough experience and developmental maturity and has grown up in an environment of love and interest, academics will take relatively little time and effort, especially in the early years. On the other hand, formal instruction without these prerequisites is almost useless and can be damaging. Such reflections helped me think of learning in a way that didn't have to include hours of structured lessons every day.

Regarding seeds, there is the familiar parable in the Gospels about the farmer who scattered seeds which fell in different environments: rocky, hard, shallow, fertile. This image of planting seeds reminds me that one can't always predict what will take root and how it will bloom. I remember reading a book about a saint to a child who seemed to be bored by it. I did not find out until years later that the seed of this saint's heroic life and death had been implanted quite deeply within the child. Another time, I started a "free writing" period right before lunch. Everyone, including me, gathered and wrote something—it didn't matter what. We sat for twenty minutes, and even the baby had crayons and paper in his high chair. Our practice was the starting point for one of the children to write a full-length novel over the course of the next two years. Much later, the free writing had evolved into an informal family Story Society.

I must admit that the planting of seeds is hard for me to carry out consistently. I am rather shy and easily discouraged, and I have trouble sharing my heart interests with others unless I am fairly sure they will be sympathetic. Kids can be quite frank in their reactions, though they are also usually hungry to know what really matters to their parents. I have tried to cultivate courage and patience in this planting and sowing. Some of the seeds don't take, but that is part of the process, too. I have tried to learn to stand back, to wait, to be sensitive to a hesitation or difficulty on the part of a child. If there is one, perhaps it is time to go back and tend the roots and soil again.

I don't always have to plant the seeds myself, I hasten to add. One of our children became interested in trees because we live in a National Forest. He studied piles of books and now has the equivalent of a field guide in his head, as well as a deep love for the trees themselves and a fondness for natural history writing. And because of our medical interlude with our sixth child, the older children learned about G-tubes and oxygen monitors—not to mention how important prayer and the communion of saints are in our day-to-day lives.

Perhaps I was being prepared to unschool by my father's example when I was a teenager. He was the medical director in a city hospital, with an impressive curriculum vitae, but he left this successful career to go back to being a general physician. He did not want to get out of touch with what had brought him to medicine in the first place, namely, the ability to heal, which to him as a Christian had an essentially spiritual component.

From my father I first learned that not everything is about production, efficiency, maximizing success, or income or product. In the homeschool world, achieving much academically or participating in a number of activities outside the home is not our measure. There can be times of plowing the ground under, seemingly quiet, hidden times that are worthwhile all the same. I suppose that Our Lord's hidden life before His time of ministry and His present appearance to us in the Tabernacle teach the same lesson.

When I was spending so much time caring for my medically fragile child, my eldest was in his high-school years. He was largely unschooled, even though he made his way through a quite rigorous curriculum. I had little time to spend helping him. He did it on his own, and our conversations pinned it together. I worried that it would not be enough, but it was. He succeeded in his college application and went to the college of his choice, where he enjoyed his studies and obtained his degree.

I learned from our experience that there is a mystery in education beyond any simple input/output equation, a mystery that unschoolers appreciate and honor. What is learned and achieved is extremely individual to the child—and directed by God. Parents and teachers can assist, but they are not the ones primarily in charge. In *Story of a Soul,* St. Thérèse explains this mystery, writing:

> Just as the sun shines simultaneously on the tall cedars and on each little flower as though it were alone on the earth, so Our Lord is occupied particularly with each soul as though there were no others like it. And just as in nature all the seasons are arranged in such a way as to make the humblest daisy bloom on a set day, in the same way, everything works out for the good of each soul. (14-15)

For a long time I was attracted to unschooling, but was unsure that it was compatible with my Catholic Faith. I was afraid it could lead to laziness or complacency on my part, or on the part of my kids. Actually, my sons and daughter have shown me that children and young adults will embark on challenging learning projects without outside requirements, and that they can meet outside requirements when it is important for them to do so. The three grown ones are serious about discerning where God is calling them, whether to a religious vocation or to some other sphere of life.

Over time I realized that it takes loving vigilance to unschool. It works with the natural bent of the child, but the process is not always easy or simple. Unschooling is a form of education inspired and carried out in love, with the goal of Love. Love is vigilant, patient, and understanding, which means being attentive to my children's unique personalities, working against the tendency to become lost in trivial tasks and unnecessary things, and trying to do as well as I can with every day God gives me. All of this takes attention and care and is far removed from laziness and complacency.

One can never be confident that one has found the perfect way; part of the joy and labor of working out our salvation is that every day provides a new beginning. Our educational endeavors have been a reflection of that truth. Unschooling has helped me in several ways to be more conscious of what is at the center of things, underneath all the plans and procedures and particulars of daily life. At the same time, it has kept me focused on those daily particulars, most specifically on trying to observe and understand my children and be a better mother to them. While unschooling has provided many benefits to my children, I too have reaped a reward. Along with my faith, it has kept me focused on the heart of things, and rooted in Love.

EPILOGUE

The Way of the Saints

Comfort, give comfort to my people, says your God.
Speak tenderly to the heart of Jerusalem . . .

—Isaiah 40:1-2

Now that you have read the refreshingly honest accounts of twelve other women, I think I need to be candid as well. Eight brave ladies have told you about their unschooling lives, and four more women have revealed the heights and depths of their homeschooling adventures. The ball is back in my court, and the time has come to be perfectly frank.

I have a confession to make. I enjoy my position as the Catholic unschooling expert. I didn't claim this title for myself; it came to me inadvertently after I wrote a book about Catholic unschooling when there were no other books on the subject. Suddenly what was *a* book became *the* book, as in "she wrote the book."

This could be embarrassing, since it is obvious to me that others are more qualified to be the experts in the field. Granted, when I wrote that book I didn't know there were other Catholic unschoolers, let alone experts, but since then I have been fortunate enough to meet more than a few. As you have seen for yourself, these are quite amazing women with an impressive array of experience. Still, I did write the book, and so *de facto* I am the professional. It's an odd position to be in, but I'm a Pollyanna type, so instead of asking, "Why me?" I have decided to sit back and use my authority to advance an agenda.

Can you guess what my agenda is? If you have been following the loose argument of the preceding pages, you won't be surprised that despite two books on the subject, my pet project is not Catholic unschooling. The program I plan to advance is more basic than any homeschooling method, yet often more challenging. It may seem radical to you or not, depending on your temperament, or perhaps your mood; if you are choleric, or having a bad day with the children, you may not go for it.

My agenda is, simply, gentleness. I call it the Way of the Saints because I want to buttress my own questionable authority with sources you can absolutely trust. I am not insisting on gentleness as the hallmark of *all* the saints; I have heard rumors that St. Jerome and St. Andre Bessette could be rather snippy. Nonetheless, I do think the virtue I advocate was, if not the dominant note of every saint, certainly characteristic of many. As we prepare to say goodbye, I would like to propose gentleness to you as a way worth pursuing.

They say you should write about what you know. I know about unschooling, because it is the atmosphere we breathe in my home, and so I write about it. I write about gentleness too, because it is what I know through my experience of the tender mercy of Jesus. I could not conclude without mentioning it, recommending it to you, portraying this mild virtue as beautifully and truly as my limited powers allow. Ultimately I will rely on St. Paul, St. Thérèse, and St. John Bosco to say well and with real authority what I want to convey.

I call gentleness a virtue; it is also a fruit of the Holy Spirit. In his letter to the Galatians, St. Paul teaches that we need to "learn to live and move in the Spirit; then there is no danger of giving way to the impulses of corrupt nature" (5:16, Knox). He goes on to list some of the effects of corrupt nature: "such things as . . . feuds, quarrels, jealousies, outbursts of anger, rivalries, dissensions, factions, spite . . ." (5:20-21, Knox). After St. Paul warns us that those who live with these vices will not inherit God's kingdom, he consoles us with the hope of a better way. He writes:

> The Spirit yields a harvest of love, joy, peace, patience, kindness, generosity, forbearance, gentleness, faith . . . (5:22-23, Knox)

Finally he exhorts us, "Since we live by the Spirit, let the Spirit be our rule of life; we must not indulge vain ambitions, envying one another and provoking one another to envy" (5:25-26, Knox).

I used to hate talking about homeschooling with other mothers. I am not an ambitious person, and yet something about those conversations felt competitive. We would tell each other what we were doing with our children, and we would each walk away feeling bad that the others were doing so much more, or at least some particular more which left us feeling inadequate or as if we were short-changing our kids. My son was doing Latin, but her son was studying biology; Joseph was into the piano, but the neighbor boy was on a baseball team. She concluded she was failing her children by not introducing a classical language and music, while I sadly realized that mine would never learn science, good sportsmanship, and teamwork.

I can still vividly recall the discouragement I felt. I was comparing myself to those around me and finding myself inferior, while actually those around me were comparing themselves to me and thinking they were the inferior ones. Spending time together was like engaging in a big judge-fest. It didn't matter that the harshest judgments were those we made on ourselves; it hurt. I am not sure precisely which of St. Paul's unattractive vices I was privy to, but I was surely not experiencing joy, peace, or gentleness;

more often I was feeling provoked to jealousy or envy. I can never keep these last two straight, but suffice it to say the result was not good.

One particular episode brought home to me the irony of such encounters which, though between friends, were generating a form of rivalry. The incident did not bear directly on homeschooling, but is a perfect example of the kind of unhealthy competition that homeschooling conversations can produce.

My eye-opening revelation took place the day I dropped in unannounced on my friend Jackie, only to find that her usually neat-as-a-pin house was a mess. Apparently, we had both always given each other at least a five-minute warning when we were planning to visit. Enough time, as you well know, to scurry about and make the place presentable. We had known each other for years, but we had each continued under the completely false impression that the other had mastered the art of living, with children, in a perpetually tidy home. It was a relief to learn that we were both simply human after all, and then, too, there is nothing more healing than laughter. We did laugh together that day as we saw the humble truth, and I smile remembering it now. But perhaps the most important result of my discovery was that I came away with a newfound kindness toward myself, knowing that it was normal to live in a home that looked, well, lived in.

I am hoping that, similarly, you will come away from this book with some extra gentleness for yourself. You have been reading about the homes of thirteen different women. Believe me, we all had our five-minute warning, and although not every messy bit got stuffed into the closet or shoved under the bed, we did attempt to show you our company manners. Do not be fooled by the veneer. We are just like you, wondering what in the world we will put together for dinner tonight. We are just like you, and not entirely sure of ourselves. We may write long books and thoughtful Internet posts proclaiming the goodness and freedom of unschooling; at the end of the day we still lie in bed exhausted and wonder if our children are learning what they should.

The great news is that none of us needs to be completely self-assured, because we have a very big heaven full of saints who are keeping an eye on us, desirous of providing a much truer assurance, and always ready to come to our aid in this valley of tears. They will be our mentors in the way of gentleness, a way which they learned from the Way Himself. Let's start with St. Thérèse, since she so explicitly promised not to forget us and has proven herself such a good friend.

Bishop Patrick Ahern published a marvelous book, *Maurice and Thérèse*, in which he assembled the correspondence between St. Thérèse and her spiritually adopted missionary brother Maurice Belliere. Maurice's letters are full of the sort of things we would say, and Thérèse's letters contain precisely the words we are longing to hear. He begins by telling her, "The Lord is sending me a hard trial . . . and I am very weak" (57). But later, after getting to know Thérèse, he is able to write,

> As you put it so well and plainly, since we are two doing the work, I am to rely fully on the Lord and on you. This is the surest way. I look upon everything you tell me as coming from Jesus Himself. I have full confidence in you and I am guided by your way, which I would like to make my own. (145)

Sadly for Maurice, Thérèse was dying. He had trouble imagining how he could get along without their continued correspondence. The words Thérèse wrote to him, explaining his advantage in her death, are a perfect explanation of the role we can count on the saints to play in our own little dramas. Listen as she speaks to our hearts.

> I have to tell you, that we don't understand Heaven in the same way. You think that, once I share in the justice and

> holiness of God, I won't be able to excuse your faults as I did when I was on earth. Are you then forgetting that I shall also share in the *infinite mercy* of the Lord? I believe that the Blessed in Heaven have great compassion for our miseries. They remember that when they were weak and mortal like us, they committed the same faults themselves and went through the same struggles, and their fraternal tenderness becomes still greater than it ever was on earth. It's on account of this that they never stop watching over us and praying for us. (209-210)

According to Thérèse's account, we can be sure of receiving her own solicitous and gentle care. She says of the saints, "Their fraternal tenderness becomes still greater than it ever was on earth." This is good news because Thérèse herself had such remarkable tenderness in her earthly life. To get some idea of Thérèse's heavenly interest in us, let us look at how she expressed her charity while still earthbound.

In her *Memoir of My Sister St. Thérèse*, Celine (Thérèse's biological sister, and also her religious sister in the Carmel) recounted Thérèse's concern for others. Celine wrote:

> One day in the Infirmary during her last illness, my sister called my attention to the soft, downy linens which the infirmarian, Sister Stanislaus, always had at hand for the benefit of her patients. "Souls should be treated with the same tender care," the Saint said, "but why is it that we forget this so frequently, and allow those about us to go on unnoticed in the endurance of sharp, interior pain? Shouldn't the spiritual needs of the soul be attended to with the same charity, with the same delicate care which we devote to our neighbor's bodily necessities? For some souls are really sick; there are many weak souls on earth, and *all* souls without exception suffer at one time or other during life. How

tenderly we should not only love them but also *show* our love for them." (130-131)

Surely we have here a saint who does not take our needs and petitions lightly. And when I consider that in her *Story of a Soul* she explains, "When I am charitable, it is Jesus alone who is acting in me" (221), when I comprehend that surely even such gentleness as hers is merely a shadow cast by Gentleness Incarnate, then I am compelled to tell you the truth, which is that you have nothing to fear.

Our Lord Himself is the King of Gentleness, entirely in love with your precious soul; He is living perpetually clothed with a body in order to present it constantly before the heavenly Father in petition for your needs. You are taken care of by the Master. He makes Himself your servant, and then, afraid that is not enough, bids you call Him Friend. And still none of this is enough for Him. He will keep giving beyond all measure.

And so, when He takes the likes of us up to heaven, for instance when He takes a twenty-four-year-old French girl to Himself, what does He do next? He draws her up onto His lap, puts all His treasures into her hands, and smiles to see her toss them down to her poor sisters and brothers still on earth. Jesus delights in the liberality of the saints, while they rejoice to bestow on us the riches He has shared with them. What a merciful God we have.

We can discern an important hierarchy of gentleness here. Just as we love God because He first loved us, so we are able to be gentle with ourselves and others because He has first been gentle with us. The saints by their intercession, their teachings, and their example contribute to our experience and understanding of gentleness. Finally, having been the recipients of so much heavenly gentleness and inspired by the Holy Spirit, we are in a position to let this divine attribute shine through us and onto those around us.

The book you are holding tells of the adventures of thirteen women as they attempt to follow the advice of St. Thérèse to trust God and be gentle. We have tried to be honest, and let you know that we are all in the same boat, one which experiences storms while Jesus sleeps. All too frequently we lose our poise, we fall apart, we are harsh with our children, we are merciless toward ourselves. Like the apostles, we sometimes panic and are desperate for Jesus to save us, but sure enough, sooner or later He wakes up, calms the wind and sea, and we know peace (and gentleness) again.

Our boat is the barque of Peter, and we can be sure that it will reach the heavenly shore intact. While we are fellow passengers, let us be gentle with one another. Let us encourage each other to be gentle with ourselves. And last but not least, let's pray that we can be gentle with the children.

I don't really know which of these three expressions of gentleness is the hardest. I fail at them all on a daily basis. I find consolation, however, in knowing I am not alone. St. Thérèse writes about feeling the same frustrations that plague us. In fact, she is so much like us that her words could be a text message sent only this morning. In her loving voice she tells us she understands and has found a way to make even our failings a new occasion for gentleness. She says:

> I have my weaknesses also, but I rejoice in them. I don't always succeed either in rising above the nothings of this earth; for example, I will be tormented by a foolish thing I said or did. Then I enter into myself, and I say: Alas, I'm still at the same place as I was formerly! But I tell myself this with great gentleness and without any sadness! It's so good to feel that one is weak and little! (*Last Conversations*, 73-74)

She speaks of a double failure which is all too familiar. First there is the foolish thing we say or do; then adding insult to injury is our disappointment in ourselves. Her solution is at once appealing and somewhat elusive. She suggests we taste the sweetness of feeling ourselves weak and little. How exactly does that help? Why is it sweet to feel weak and little? Wouldn't progress in the way of perfection be a more lasting and positive resolution? We may be used to our littleness, but what about spiritual growth?

Thérèse answers our questions with the wisdom that comes from the Holy Spirit. She simply reminds us that God is merciful Love. Therefore, our miseries satisfy Him in a way our perfection could not. Weakness and littleness provide the proper object for His infinite mercy. The smaller we are and the greater our needs, the lower God must stoop to save us, and thus the more God's compassion is glorified. St. Paul said it best, or rather Jesus said it best, as St. Paul writes to the Corinthians:

> He told me, "My grace is enough for thee; my strength finds its full scope in thy weakness." More than ever, then, I delight to boast of the weaknesses that humiliate me, so that the strength of Christ may enshrine itself in me. (2 Corinthians 12:9-10, Knox)

St. Paul's testimony is powerful and his logic compelling, but we may fear that such a strong dependence on our poverty will tempt us to presumption. St. Thérèse is not surprised at our caution. She encountered a great deal of resistance from the novices she advised and from other sisters in her monastery. In the face of every objection, however, she was and is adamant that the way of spiritual childhood—her way of always remaining little—is safe. She even promised her novices before she died,

> If I lead you into error with my Little Way of Love, be not afraid that I shall permit you to follow it for any length of time. I would soon re-appear after my death and tell you to take another road. But if I do not return, believe me when I tell you that we never have too much confidence in the good Lord. (*Complete Spiritual Doctrine of St. Thérèse*, 8)

Far from retracting her teaching, St. Thérèse has been spending her heaven doing good upon earth in order to entice us into the Love of God. Her shower of roses gives us divine assurance that her way is authentic. She suggests we make the most of our weakness, turning our falls into appeals for Love.

In addition to St. Thérèse, another saint who effectively conveys the gentle love of God is St. John Bosco. He also specializes in exhorting us to be mirrors of that love to our children. Thus far I have been concerned with illustrating the beautiful necessity of practicing gentleness toward ourselves, but now let us return with St. John to a consideration of gentleness toward our children.

John Bosco is a favorite among Catholic unschoolers, who admire his manner of dealing with the seven hundred boys he taught and with whom he lived. (And you thought your family was large!) He was a priest and educator who lived in Italy in the mid to late 1800s—you might know him as Don Bosco. His motto was "*amo et fac quod vis*": love, and do what you will. A biographer comments, "Hence, his easy manner, free of anxiety and marked by the full freedom of the child of God" (*The Educational Philosophy of St. John Bosco*, 46).

Unschoolers have adopted Don Bosco as a patron because that easy manner, lack of anxiety, and experience of the full freedom of the child of God are exactly what we desire. Moreover, we hope to obtain these things by living as he did. John Bosco was an educator, and so are we. What advice does he have for us? He tells us simply, "Without confidence and love, there can be no true education" (*Educational Philosophy*, 52). A statement with which St. Thérèse and John Holt would enthusiastically agree.

As with St. Thérèse, I do not mean to claim St. John Bosco as the exclusive property of unschoolers. The saints belong to us all, and we to them, united intimately in the nonexclusive Mystical Body of Christ. We take this or that saint as our guiding star on account of an ineffable attraction the Holy Spirit inspires; more concretely, we often recognize that a saint lived by the very principles we hold dear, or personifies the virtues and gifts we want to animate our lives.

With St. John Bosco, unschoolers have noticed that he educated according to the same principles we embrace. Again, the principles themselves may not be exclusive to unschooling, but they are foundational to it. Confidence. Love. Gentleness. No wonder I love unschooling. It's so simple I don't even have to remember complete sentences.

In Don Bosco we see once more God's amazing gentleness and compassion. This saint brings the motherly tenderness of the Church to bear on education, thus reassuring our anxious hearts. He understood "that education takes time, that time must be provided for a gradual response from children" (*Educational Philosophy*, 52). Aah, take a deep breath. It does not all have to happen today. And another deep breath, because it does not have to get done this year. We have time.

The following paragraphs are excerpts from a letter St. John wrote near the end of his life to his Salesians, priests and brothers in the order he founded. They were called Salesians after the saint of gentleness *par excellence*, St. Francis de Sales. John Bosco loved this saint, finding inspiration in a man who had conquered his own choleric and impatient disposition in order to "attract souls to Christ, because more flies are caught by a spoonful of honey than by a barrel of vinegar" (*Educational Philosophy*, 158).

We, the authors, join with St. John Bosco and St. Thérèse in praying that you will discover your happiest way of homeschooling, a way that fills your lives with the gifts of the Holy Spirit. By all means remember that there is no rush; God has all the time in the world. For now, we offer a few last words on gentleness from a saint who, like us, spent nearly every waking moment surrounded by children. St. John writes:

It seems to me that the words of the Holy Gospel which speak to us of the Divine Savior come down from Heaven to earth to gather together all the children of God scattered all over the world, could be applied literally to the young people of our times. They constitute the most vulnerable yet valuable section of human society. We base our hopes for the future on them, and they are not of their nature depraved . . . .These young people truly have need of some kind person who will take care of them, work with them, guide them in virtue, keep them away from harm.

When teachers are thought of as superior and no longer as fathers, brothers and friends, they are feared and little loved. And so if you want everyone to be of one heart and soul again for the love of Jesus you must break down this fatal barrier of mistrust, and replace it with a spirit of confidence in you.

How then are we to set about breaking down this barrier? By a friendly informal relationship with the young, especially in recreation. You cannot have love without this familiarity, and where this is not evident there can be no confidence. If you want to be loved, you must make it clear that you love. Jesus Christ made Himself little with the little ones and bore our weaknesses. He is our master in the matter of the friendly approach.

In general, the system we ought to adopt is called Preventive, which consists in so disposing the hearts of our students that they ought to be willing to do what we ask of them without need of external violence. I would like to think that coercive means are never to be used, but only and exclusively those suggested by patience and charity. . . . If therefore I want to be a true father to these children, then I must have a father's heart, and not turn to repression or punishment without reason and without justice, and only in the manner of one who does so under duress, and for the sake of duty.

How often in my long career have I had to convince myself of this great truth! It is certainly easier to lose one's temper than to be patient; threaten young people rather than reason with them. I would say that it better suits our lack of patience and our pride to punish those who resist us, rather than bear with them firmly and with kindness . . . [but] if we want to know how to command, let us be careful to first learn how to obey, and let us set out first and foremost to make ourselves loved rather than feared . . .

In certain more serious moments it is more useful to turn to God, to humble oneself before Him, than to let loose a torrent of words which, on the one hand only harms the one who hears them, on the other hand does nothing for the one who deserved them. When we see our efforts prove ineffectual, and we have only thorns and brambles to show for all our labors, believe me, we must put it down to defective methods of discipline.

God is not in the whirlwind, which St. Teresa interpreted as, "Let nothing disturb you." Our gentle St. Francis de Sales used to say, "I am afraid to lose in a quarter of an hour that little gentleness that I have managed to put together drop by drop over twenty years." What's the point of talking to someone who is not listening? One day he was reproached for having dealt with excessive gentleness with a young man who had seriously offended his mother. He replied, "This young man was not capable of gaining anything from any rebuke of mine, because his poor attitude had deprived him of reason and common sense. A harsh correction would have done nothing for him, and would have done me a lot of harm, causing me to act like those people who drown trying to rescue another."

Young people often need convincing that we have confidence in their ability to improve, and feel there is a kindly hand to help them. You can get more with a friendly look, with a word of encouragement that gives his heart new courage, than you can with repeated blame, which serves only to upset, and weaken enthusiasm. Using this system, I have seen real conversions among those one would otherwise have believed impossible. All youngsters have their off-days—you have had them yourselves! Heaven help us if we do not try to help them to get through them without trouble. Sometimes simply having them understand you do not think they acted from malice is enough to ensure they do not fall again into the same fault.

Remember that education is a matter of the heart, of which God is the sole master, and we will be unable to achieve anything unless God teaches us, and puts the key in our hands. Let us strive to make ourselves loved, and we will see the doors of many hearts open with great ease, and join with us in singing praises and blessing of Him who wished to make Himself our model, our way, our example in everything, but especially in the education of the young. Pray for me, and believe me, Your loving father and friend,

Fr John Bosco
Feast of St Francis of Sales 1883

Appendices

APPENDIX ONE

A Philosopher's Perspective

Tony Andres

Anthony Andres is a graduate of Thomas Aquinas College with a Ph.D. in philosophy from the University of Notre Dame, where he wrote his dissertation under the late Dr. Ralph McInerny. Tony taught philosophy and a smattering of other subjects at Christendom College for fourteen years; he currently teaches in the integrated Great Books program of Thomas Aquinas College. He is the author of several philosophical articles, a college logic textbook, and an unfinished children's novel about the adventures of Boethius.

> *No free person should learn anything like a slave.*
> *Forced bodily labor does no harm to the body,*
> *but nothing taught by force stays in the soul.*
>
> —Plato, *The Republic*

In the fall of 1970 I entered the classroom at St. Aloysius Gonzaga School in Cheektowaga, New York, to begin my first semester of kindergarten. And I never really left. True, I'm past kindergarten now, but my life has been divided into semesters ever since, first when I was a student and now that I am a teacher. Consequently it might seem strange for me to be an advocate of homeschooling in its most radical form, unschooling. But when Suzie suggested that I write an essay for this book, I jumped at the chance. I want Catholic parents to know that, while unschooling is not for every family or every child, it is an option perfectly compatible with the perennial philosophy promoted by the Catholic Church.

If we are going to justify it philosophically, we will have to begin by finding out what unschooling is and stating the obvious objections to it. Our next step will be to examine the educational principles offered by Aristotle and St. Thomas Aquinas. We will use those principles to see how unschooling, rightly understood, is a legitimate educational option for some families and students.

In *Teach Your Own, The John Holt Book of Unschooling*, Patrick Farenga defines unschooling as "allowing children as much freedom to learn in the world as their parents can comfortably bear" (238). A good account as far as it goes, and helpful, but for our purposes here, let's aim at an even more precise notion. The very form of the word tells us something: *un-schooling* will be the opposite of *schooling*.

I remember my own schooldays vividly. I was dropped off every weekday at 8:20 A.M. at the elementary school and picked up at 2:30 P.M. During the day everyone in my class studied the same subjects at the same time according to the same pace, and we were taught by adults who had no other role in our lives. We received grades on every piece of work, good grades rewarding us for learning well, bad grades punishing us for not learning. Uniformity, rigidity, rewards and punishments—these capture my school experience.

The method most opposed to this would open all times and places to learning. It would use everyone in the learner's life as a teacher, would adjust itself to the interests and abilities of the learner, and would allow learning to occur for its own sake.

Unschooling, then, is the method of education which does not separate learning from the rest of the child's life according to time, place, or persons. It allows the child to learn according to his interests and abilities and makes the desire to know, rather than fear of punishment, the primary motivation for learning.

And so unschooling is not the same as homeschooling. Homeschooling parents often designate a separate room and time for instruction, using a predetermined curriculum to push learning along at a set pace. They reward and punish their children for their performance and are really replicating most of the conditions of school, only placing the process in the home. They homeschool, but do not unschool. In contrast, parents who unschool might very well have their children take advantage of courses offered at a school. As long as the parents disregard grades and allow their children to focus on learning for the sake of knowing, they are bringing unschooling into the school. The essence of unschooling is not the staying away from school buildings, but making education hinge on the desire for knowledge, rather than on rewards and punishments.

But it is not obvious that unschooling as we have just described it is a method that a Catholic parent can accept. The Church teaches us that we are all born with original sin, and that its consequence is a tendency toward disorder in our desires. In particular, one might object that children don't want to learn what they need to know, and if their parents do not force them to study, they will never learn these things. If this objection is true, unschooling would be not so much a method of education as the abdication of parental responsibility.

I entirely appreciate the force of the objection, but I am confident we can answer it. We only need to look carefully at the educational principles propounded within the school of perennial philosophy, whose chief figures are St. Thomas Aquinas and Aristotle. I do not argue that they would mandate unschooling, but I do think they would support it. St. Thomas and Aristotle both clearly affirm the following four educational principles:

1. Education should be for the good of the learner.
2. All men by nature desire to know.
3. The learner is the principal agent in learning.
4. Different learners are fitted to learn different things at different times.

I think the acceptability of unschooling clearly follows from these principles.

Before we wade into the argument, however, I want to clear away a common misconception. Catholic parents think a lot about preparing children for getting to heaven, which of course is most important, but we think less about preparing them for happiness in this life. And yet what prepares them for happiness in heaven is living happy lives on earth. By *happy life*, I do not mean a life devoid of suffering and devoted to pleasure, but a life that truly fulfills the deepest desires of our human nature.

When St. Thomas writes about the natural moral law, he does not think of it as a painful burden, as God spoiling our chances for happiness in this life; on the contrary, he sees the natural law as a set of instructions from our Maker that direct us toward achieving real happiness, both here and hereafter. A similar line of thought leads Aristotle to define happiness as the activity of the soul according to virtue (*Nicomachean Ethics*, Bk. 1, Ch. 7). Happiness, even in this life, is inseparable from moral virtue. Moreover, obedience to the revealed precepts of the New Law makes us happy in an even higher way than the natural law could. From reflections such as these, it becomes clear that our job as parents is to prepare our children for happiness in the next life by directing them toward true happiness in this one.

Which brings me back to the first principle mentioned above, namely, that education should be directed to the good of the learner. That good, as I have just argued, is the happiness of the learner, both in this life and in the next. Consequently, the education of each child should aim at his happiness.

This might seem self-evident, but I remember some of my schoolteachers implying just the opposite. They believed the world to be a hard place and consequently saw school as the training ground for the misery of life in the job market. We were being trained for jobs, and employers couldn't care less whether what we learned contributed to our happiness; they only wanted it to contribute to their profits. We would have to play along because the employers were going to pay us. If we learned well enough, we could get jobs that gave us extra money for the activities that really make life worthwhile, or we might even become the employers rather than employees. In any case, these teachers thought that what we learned in school was not something that would make us happy.

Parents, even Catholic parents, can make a similar mistake. We can push our children to succeed, partly because we think it is good for them, but partly because their success reflects well on us. If we let this happen we are acting more like employers than parents, when as parents we should be content to give each child the kind of education that will best promote his own happiness. That education is for the sake of the educated, not the educator or anyone else, is the first principle implicit in the perennial philosophy.

The second principle is enunciated by Aristotle at the beginning of his *Metaphysics*, where he writes, "All men by nature desire to know." He goes on to explain more precisely what he means:

> An indication of this is the delight we take in our senses; and above all others in the sense of sight. For not only with a view to action, but even when we are not going to do anything, we prefer seeing (one might say) to everything

> else. The reason is that this, most of all the senses, makes us know and brings to light many differences between things. (Bk. 1, Ch. 1)

Aristotle's formula implies at least two things. First, the desire to know is present in all men without exception, as is seen in the most basic kind of knowing, sense knowledge; no one fails to want to see things. Second, we desire to know even when we receive no further advantage from it. That is, knowledge is good in itself, desirable for its own sake as well as for how it helps us achieve other goods. Again our desire to see makes this clear; even when our looking at something is of no use to us, we still like to look at it.

I am sure a number of teachers and parents would dispute that children naturally desire to know. Children usually hate to study, and so we think that children would never bother to learn anything unless we forced them to. In *How Children Fail* John Holt points out the fallacy in this argument. Very small children and babies are the most eager learners of all. They investigate everything and want to do everything for themselves. In fact, they learn a tremendous amount in their first three years, prior to any schooling.

How are the youngest children different from schoolchildren? They learn what they are ready to learn, when and in the way they are ready to learn it. Holt argues in *How Children Fail* and elsewhere that it is not that children lose their desire for knowledge, but that teachers try to teach them the wrong things at the wrong time or in the wrong way. If we could find a way to match the abilities and interests of students with the subjects being taught, we would still find them eager learners. The desire to know is natural, but the way we teach can stifle natural inclinations.

And so Aristotle would deny, as John Holt does, that children must be forced to learn. St. Thomas Aquinas goes even further. In his disputed question *On the Teacher* (*On Truth*, q. 11) he argues that the mind of the student is always and necessarily the chief active cause of learning, and that the teacher is at best a helping cause. This is the third educational principle listed above. Let's consider this critical point a little more deeply.

We all know that our first knowledge comes through the five external senses and that while we might be taught to use our senses better, no one can teach us to sense something, simply speaking. I can't be taught to see the color red; I either see it, or, if I am blind or color-blind, I don't. Since sense knowledge grounds intellectual knowledge, it's clear that our most basic knowledge cannot be taught.

In fact, our minds are never simply passive, even when we are being taught. When the teacher is showing us that something is true, he has to show how it follows from more basic truths that we already know. We have to follow his argument actively, seeing for ourselves the connections he points out. And we have to see the connection that the more basic truths have to sense experience. The teacher cannot pour knowledge into our heads; he can only point out the connections of new facts to what we already know. When the student is not active in his learning, all the teacher can hope for is opinion, not knowledge.

My experience with the Pythagorean theorem, $a^2 + b^2 = c^2$, illustrates the truth of this principle. By my senior year of high school, I had gotten A's in the most difficult high-school math courses and had won an interschool math competition, and yet, though I used the formula regularly, I had never seen a proof of the Pythagorean theorem. I never even knew what the theorem really said. That is, I did not know that a^2, b^2, and c^2 represented the geometrical squares drawn on sides *a*, *b*, and *c* of the right triangle. I thought that a^2 was just the number that measured that side multiplied by itself. I had used the formula constantly, but I only had an opinion, a belief, that it was true.

Later, in college I actually saw the proof of the Pythagorean theorem; it was then that I finally *knew* the theorem. The proof worked because it appealed to facts that I already knew. It deduced the theorem from pre-existent knowledge. Without appealing to those underlying facts, even a proof would not have given me knowledge of the formula. My high-school math teachers tried to pour knowledge into my head, but they really only gave me an opinion about something that I did not understand. In college my teachers helped my mind look at the matter in the right way, so I could see the truth for myself.

Of course, this principle that learning has to be active needs to be applied in different ways to different subjects. We do not learn the Faith by seeing for ourselves. We cannot see that God is a Trinity, so it has to be revealed to us, and our belief always rests on the authority of the Church. But that does not mean that in learning the Faith our mind is purely passive. The doctrines of the Faith are presented in words, and we can't understand what they mean without actively understanding those words. Even here the mind of the student must be active in grasping the truth, to whatever degree that is possible in each case.

Now we come to our fourth principle. Because the mind of the student is necessarily the principal agent in learning, a child can't learn simply anything right away. His mind needs to take in one kind of knowledge before it can handle a higher kind. For example, it is obvious that we can't teach nuclear physics to a six-year-old; he has to learn a lot more elementary facts before he can even begin to learn basic physics. Learning has to happen in a certain order, an order not so much tied to the subject but to the capacities of the human mind.

Not only do some subjects have to come before others, but also different children have different levels of natural ability that determine what they are ready to learn and when. I am not merely saying that some children are brighter than others, although that is true, but that even children of equal intelligence, because of differences in temperament, are more apt to learn in one area than another.

The most obvious example is the difference between girls and boys. Girls tend to be more mature than boys of the same age and tend to be much more verbally adept. Consequently, it is very likely that a girl will be able to learn a verbal skill which a boy of the same age will be incapable of learning.

I think that temperamental differences can be as important as differences between boys and girls. Some minds are more creative, others more analytical, some incline more toward certainties, others toward doubtful matters, and these differences will affect not only how and when a student learns, but also what he is capable of learning.

Trying to teach higher mathematics to artists will be just as frustrating as trying to teach the mathematician to write poetry. In each case, the student who is not temperamentally suited for a subject will be unlikely to benefit from more than an introductory study of it. Consequently, the effort to make every student study the same subjects at the same age and same pace is bound to do more harm than good.

Let's review the four principles as we've seen them thus far. First, we saw that education is for the good of the child, which means that what a child learns should be taught to him for the sake of his happiness, not for the benefit of the one teaching. This is how the education which a parent is bound to provide for his child differs from the training an employer provides for his workers. Second, we saw that all children are natural learners, and that what may seem to be an aversion to learning in them actually results from how we try to teach them. Third, we saw that the mind of the student is always the principal active cause of learning. Teachers cannot make the process occur, but can only help it along. Finally, we saw not only that children learning the same things are often ready to learn them at different ages, but also that particular children are more suited to learn some things rather than others. A fixed curriculum that goes beyond the basics will not work for every child. We will need to use these four principles to judge the legitimacy of unschooling.

In fact, it is not hard to see why unschooling is a legitimate option for the homeschooling parent, Catholic or not. First, unschooling by definition suits the instruction of the child to that child's present interests and abilities, and so it respects the fourth principle, that each child learns various things at varying paces. And for the same reason, unschooling respects the first principle, that education is for the good of the child. It directs education toward the happiness of the child and the adult he will become, so that he has the opportunity to develop and use his natural talents and is not frustrated by a demand to develop abilities for which he is not suited.

But I think that we especially see the excellence of unschooling when we look at the second and third principles of education, that all men desire to know and that the mind of the student is the principal active cause of learning. The parents of the unschooled child trust that their child really wants to learn, and so they can leave aside the external rewards and punishments schools use to make children study. The parent is confident the child will be able to learn largely on his own, because the parent knows the child's mind is made to learn. Not that the child never needs instruction. Rather, the child will want instruction when he needs it, and such instruction will be an aid to what the child is already doing, not the imposition of an alien task. Unschooling respects the different minds of different children and helps each child to fulfill his potential to learn.

A point to keep in mind is that children learn best by imitation. They learn to talk by imitating our speech and to speak grammatically from our correct speech. If we are afraid that our children will never want to read, we should reflect on our own lives. Do *we* read? Do we read to our children? Do our children see that we enjoy reading, that we see reading as something necessary for our own happiness? If the answer to these questions is yes, then we can trust our children to want to learn to read.

You might think I am saying that unschooling is the best or even the only method of education for every child, but that would be taking my argument too far. There are good schools and good teachers who respect these principles, and there are many children whose abilities line up well with the standard school curriculum. Many children also like the structure and social opportunities that school gives them. Even among homeschooled children and parents, some will be comfortable with more direction and structure than others. I think there should be plenty of options for educating children, and parents should be free to explore them all for each child. My contention here is that for some parents and some children at some times, unschooling will be the best educational method.

Before I end, I want to mention how my argument differs from that implicit in some unschooling literature. That literature takes freedom, understood as an almost complete lack of restriction, to be the greatest good for human beings. It then makes the quick deduction that the only legitimate way of educating children is unschooling because unschooling allows children the most freedom. I reject this argument because I reject the principle that freedom is the greatest good. True, unschooling does allow the child a large measure of freedom in learning, but that freedom is a means to learning, not an end in itself. Parents still need to discipline their children; to restrict freedom when it is conducive to the true good of the child. The freedom that accompanies unschooling should not be a simple lack of restraint, but a real freedom, that is, the opportunity for each child to learn in the way that best brings about his true happiness.

APPENDIX TWO

Books We Love

I'm 30 years old, but I read at the 34-year-old level.

—Dana Carvey

I love books, but I must admit that I do not always love book lists. I want to tell you about my favorite books and hear about yours, but once we compile a list, the sheer number of titles and authors can overwhelm me. I concluded my first book with an appendix listing my most beloved books and authors. There are books I have discovered and come to love since then; add to my new recommendations those of the other contributors to this volume, and you see how this appendix could become unwieldy.

In order to keep our recommendations simple and useful, I asked the ladies and my husband to name just their most cherished books on homeschooling and on the spiritual life. With so many irresistible books out there, our categories grew to include St. Thérèse, unschooling, homeschooling, books on books, children's books that inspire learning, education, parenting, and spiritual books. We had fun exchanging titles, and we are happy to offer our favorites to you. The entries are listed by author and title. Some of the books are out of print, but the Internet, your local library, and neighborhood booksellers can help you locate them.

In order to help you avoid the perplexity and hesitation I often feel at the suggestion of too many wonderful books all at once, let me single out for you my top two recommended titles. That way if you never do more than glance at the lists of books we love, you can still go away with two initial suggestions that just might change your life.

The first book I hope you get for your bedside table or to take with you to church is *I Believe in Love* by Fr. Jean d'Elbée. This wonderful book, published by Sophia Institute Press, is full of encouragement and consolation. It is a collection of retreat conferences given by Fr. d'Elbée on the teaching of St. Thérèse. He speaks of the childlike confidence that Thérèse lived, and he illustrates through many examples how such confidence can and should be ours. He writes in Chapter 1:

> I assure you, we are bathed in love and mercy. We each have a Father, a Brother, a Friend, a Spouse of our soul, Center and King of our hearts, Redeemer and Savior, bent down over us like the apple of his eye, who said, "I will have mercy and not sacrifice, for I have not come to call the just, but sinners," a Jesus haunted by the desire to save us by all means, who has opened Heaven under our feet. (23-24)

I Believe in Love is the best book I know of about the Little Way, and it has moved many, many people to a better understanding of God's kindness and mercy. I highly recommend it.

My second suggestion is that you become acquainted with the books of Conrad Baars, a Thomistic psychiatrist who died in 1981. He was a Catholic who served the Church by writing for priests, religious, and laity; treating patients from all walks of life; speaking around the country; and traveling back and forth to his Dutch homeland to collaborate with Dr. Anne Terruwe. He wrote several books to share the wisdom he had learned from the philosophy of

St. Thomas Aquinas, and I am often saddened and perplexed that his brilliant work is so little known.

I tell you about Dr. Baars because his writings are an irreplaceable gift which I want you to have the joy of receiving. In particular, I suggest his book *Feeling and Healing Your Emotions*, in which he presents a straightforward summary of the most important truths he has gleaned from St. Thomas.

So, again, I most highly recommend *I Believe in Love*, and I encourage you to get to know Conrad Baars.

Mike Aquilina says in his introduction to Maureen Wittmann's book of book lists *For the Love of Literature*, "Reading is a pleasure and a joy; it's an escape and a diversion; it's edifying and inspiring. But, when it's really good, it's still more than that. It's all about love" (10). We agree wholeheartedly. We offer you these authors and their books with a prayer that God will use them to fill your hearts and homes with love.

One brief caveat: We begin our list on unschooling books with several by John Holt, the author who introduced many of us to unschooling. He was a remarkable man, a superb writer, and a great observer of children. We do not, however, simply endorse all that he wrote. Instead we direct you to the particular books of his that we have listed, for these we do recommend. And now, to the books.

The great thing is to be always reading
but not to get bored—
treat it not like work, more as a vice!
Your book bill ought to be
your biggest extravagance.

—C. S. Lewis

Books We Love

ON ST. THÉRÈSE

St. Thérèse of Lisieux
Story of a Soul
Her Last Conversations

Fr. Jean C. J. D'Elbée
I Believe in Love

Pere Liagre
A Retreat with St. Thérèse

Sister Genevieve of the Holy Face (Celine Martin)
My Sister St. Thérèse (reprint of *A Memoir of My Sister St. Thérèse*)
The Spirit of St. Thérèse de l'Enfant Jesus

Patrick Ahern
Maurice and Thérèse: The Story of a Love

Francois Jamart, O.C.D.
Complete Spiritual Doctrine of St. Thérèse of Lisieux

John Nelson
The Little Way of Saint Thérèse of Lisieux

ON UNSCHOOLING

John Holt

How Children Fail

How Children Learn

Learning All the Time

What Do I Do Monday?

Instead of Education

Never Too Late

John Holt and Patrick Farenga

Teach Your Own: The John Holt Book of Homeschooling

Jan and Jason Hunt (editors)

The Unschooling Unmanual

Alison McKee

Homeschooling Our Children, Unschooling Ourselves

Nancy Wallace

Better Than School

Kendall Hailey

The Day I Became an Autodidact

Patricia Joudry

And the Children Played

Teri J. Brown

Christian Unschooling

Mary Griffith

The Unschooling Handbook

Rue Kream

Parenting a Free Child: An Unschooled Life

❧

ON CATHOLIC HOMESCHOOLING

Suzie Andres

Homeschooling with Gentleness: A Catholic Discovers Unschooling

Laura Berquist

Designing Your Own Classical Curriculum

Mary Kay Clark

Catholic Home Schooling

Elizabeth Foss

Real Learning: Education in the Heart of the Home

Alice Gunther

Haystack Full of Needles: A Catholic Home Educator's Guide to Socialization

Kimberly Hahn and Mary Hasson

Catholic Education: Homeward Bound

Susie Lloyd

Please Don't Drink the Holy Water!
Bless Me, Father, For I Have Kids

Maureen Wittmann and Rachel Mackson (editors)

The Catholic Homeschool Companion
A Catholic Homeschool Treasury

ON HOMESCHOOLING

Karen Andreola

A Charlotte Mason Companion

Pocketful of Pinecones

Lessons at Blackberry Inn

Andrew Campbell

The Latin-Centered Curriculum

Sally Clarkson

Educating the Wholehearted Child

David and Micki Colfax

Homeschooling for Excellence

David Guterson

Family Matters: Why Homeschooling Makes Sense

Mary Hood

The Relaxed Home School

The Joyful Home Schooler

Taking the Frustration out of Math (booklet)

Charlotte Mason

Charlotte Mason's Original Homeschooling Series

Susan Schaeffer Macauley

For the Children's Sake

Raymond and Dorothy Moore

The Successful Homeschool Family Handbook

Better Late Than Early

Home Grown Kids

Rebecca Rupp

Home Learning Year by Year

❧

ON BOOKS

Jan Bloom
Who Should We Then Read?

Cay Gibson
A Picture Perfect Childhood

Helene Hanff
84, Charing Cross Road

Gladys Hunt
Honey for a Child's Heart
Honey for a Teen's Heart
Honey for a Woman's Heart

Michael D. O'Brien
A Landscape with Dragons

Joseph Pearce
Literary Converts

Daniel Pennac
Better Than Life

Jim Trelease
The Read Aloud Handbook

Maureen Wittmann
For the Love of Literature

CHILDREN'S BOOKS THAT INSPIRE LEARNING

Francis J. Finn, S.J.
Facing Danger

Dorothy Canfield Fisher
Understood Betsy

Sterling North
Rascal

Marcus Pfister
The Happy Hedgehog

Patricia Polacco
Thank You, Mr. Falker

Eleanor H. Porter
Pollyanna

Gene Stratton-Porter
Freckles

Johanna Spyri
Heidi

Booth Tarkington
Penrod: His Complete Story
Seventeen

Stephanie S. Tolan
Surviving the Applewhites

E. B. White
The Trumpet of the Swan

❧

ON EDUCATION

St. Thomas Aquinas
On the Teacher (available in *Aquinas: Selected Writings*, edited by Ralph McInerny)

Thomas Armstrong
In Their Own Way: Discovering and Encouraging Your Child's Multiple Intelligences

Stratford Caldecott
Beauty for Truth's Sake: On the Re-enchantment of Education

Sofia Cavalletti
The Religious Potential of the Child: Experiencing Scripture and Liturgy with Young Children

Howard Gardner
Multiple Intelligences

John Taylor Gatto
Dumbing Us Down
The Underground History of American Education
Weapons of Mass Instruction

John Morrison
The Educational Philosophy of St. John Bosco

Frank Smith
The Book of Learning and Forgetting

Shinichi Suzuki
Nurtured by Love

James S. Taylor
Poetic Knowledge: The Recovery of Education

❧

ON PARENTING

Becky A. Bailey

Easy to Love, Difficult to Discipline

I Love You Rituals

Ross Campbell

How to Really Love Your Teenager

Mary Sheedy Kurcinka

Raising Your Spirited Child

Cathleen Lewis

Rex

Robert J. MacKenzie

Setting Limits with Your Strong-Willed Child

Gordon Neufeld and Gabor Maté

Hold on To Your Kids: Why Parents Need to Matter More Than Peers

Gregory K. Popcak

Parenting with Grace

Fr. William Virtue

Mother and Infant

❧

ON THE SPIRITUAL LIFE

Conrad Baars

Born Only Once
Feeling and Healing Your Emotions
Psychic Wholeness and Healing (with Anna Terruwe)
Healing the Unaffirmed
Doctor of the Heart

St. Francis de Sales

Thy Will Be Done: Letters to Persons in the World
Introduction to the Devout Life

St. Teresa of Avila

The Way of Perfection
The Book of Her Life

St. John of the Cross

The Spiritual Canticle

Blessed Elizabeth of the Trinity

Complete Works of Elizabeth of the Trinity

Michael Aquilina III

St. Jude, A Friend in Hard Times

Mike Aquilina

Fire of God's Love: 120 Reflections on the Eucharist

Jean-Pierre de Caussade

Abandonment to Divine Providence

G. K. Chesterton

Orthodoxy
Brave New Family

Thomas Dubay

Fire Within

Karen Edmisten

The Rosary: Keeping Company with Jesus and Mary

Through the Year with Mary: 365 Reflections

John Janaro

Never Give Up: My Life and God's Mercy

Monsignor Ronald Knox

Retreat for Lay People

The Creed in Slow Motion

Fr. Joseph Langford

Mother Teresa's Secret Fire

Mother Teresa: In the Shadow of Our Lady

Elisabeth Leseur

The Secret Diary of Elisabeth Leseur

C. S. Lewis

Surprised by Joy

Luis Martinez

When Jesus Sleeps

Thomas Merton

The Seven Storey Mountain

Luis de la Palma

The Sacred Passion

Jacques Philippe

Time for God

Searching For and Maintaining Peace

❧

MAGAZINES

Magnificat: A monthly missal that includes the daily Mass, a variation on Morning Prayer and Evening Prayer from the Divine Office, daily meditations, and more; very highly recommended.
www.magnificat.com

mater et magistra: A seasonal magazine filled with resources and encouragement for Catholic homeschooling moms. Subscribe at www.materetmagistramagazine.org where you can also download selected articles from back issues.

Growing Without Schooling: John Holt and company's original newsletter/magazine. Although GWS is no longer in print, you can get the first twelve issues as a one volume large format paperback book from www.fun-books.com, where you will also find some back issues still available.

Home Education Magazine: Articles on homeschooling, including many on unschooling; the publisher maintains an informative website where you can browse or subscribe at:
www.homeedmag.com

Life Learning Magazine: A digital magazine. Along with subscription information, the publisher's website offers essays on unschooling and selected articles from back issues.
www.lifelearningmagazine.com

APPENDIX THREE

Our Internet Places

Friendship arises . . . when two or more of the companions discover that they have in common some insight or interest or even taste which the others do not share and which, till that moment, each believed to be his own unique treasure (or burden). The typical expression of opening Friendship would be something like, "What! You too? I thought I was the only one."

—C. S. Lewis, *The Four Loves*

If you have felt lonely in your homeschooling or unschooling life, hopefully this book has convinced you that you are not actually alone. Now that you've become acquainted with the thirteen women here, we would like you to know that there are many more of us writing and lurking in the virtual hallways where we first met, on the Internet.

To help you locate kindred spirits and continue to receive reassurance, we have listed our blogs, a couple of Yahoo groups where you can find us, and a handful of websites that provide helpful information on unschooling and homeschooling.

I encourage those looking for unschooling support to join the Yahoo group UnschoolingCatholics at groups.yahoo.com/group/UnschoolingCatholics/. This email discussion group is a forum for over two hundred Catholic unschoolers, and is full of prayer support, moral support, information, advice, questions and answers, and every so often a book discussion. Conversations range from "What does your unschooling look like today?" to "How do you unschool math?" Most of this book's contributors are members, and some of us chime in frequently. The charity that reigns on the board is inspiring.

We hope, too, you will get to know some of us better through the blogs and websites where you can find our latest writings. I happily discovered the existence of other Catholic unschoolers through the Internet, and I am grateful. It is much more fun to be countercultural when you know you are not the only one.

Online Resources

OUR BLOGS

http://unschoolingcatholics.blogspot.com

Leonie's

http://livingwithoutschool.blogspot.com

Willa's

http://quotidianmoments.blogspot.com

Karen's

http://karenedmisten.blogspot.com

Melissa's

www.melissawiley.com/blog/

Faith's

http://strewing.blogspot.com

Beate and Sabine's

www.catholic-mommas.xanga.com/

Sabine's (for Michael)

www.caringbridge.org/visit/lovemichael/

Maria's

http://tater-tots-and-ladybug-love.blogspot.com

YAHOO GROUPS/EMAIL LISTS

Unschooling Catholics Yahoo group (where you can find many of our contributors)

http://groups.yahoo.com/group/UnschoolingCatholics/

Catholic Classical Education Yahoo group

http://groups.yahoo.com/group/cce/

College 4 Catholic Homeschoolers Ongoing forthright discussions about colleges by parents and admissions counselors

http://groups.yahoo.com/groups/College4CathHS/

WEBSITES PERTAINING TO HOMESCHOOLING AND UNSCHOOLING

Hillside Education is the publisher of this and many other fine books for the discriminating Catholic homeschooler. Also publisher of the magazine *mater et magistra*, Hillside maintains a site rich in appeal to a wide range of homeschooling types.

www.hillsideeducation.com

The 4Real forums, "education in the context of life," provide a place for Catholic homeschoolers to discuss all sorts of topics.

http://4real.thenetsmith.com

Fun-books.com is where you can find back issues of *Growing Without Schooling*, as well as many other wonderful unschooling books and resources.

http://fun-books.com

Patrick Farenga is president of Holt Associates. He was a colleague and close friend of John Holt's and has continued to work, speak, and write on unschooling and education. Pat's website provides information on free learning resources for adults and children, the latest news about homeschooling around the world, and more. He also maintains a second website "to keep John Holt's own ideas and words available."

www.patfarenga.com
www.holtgws.com

APPENDIX FOUR

A Passel of Prayers

Hear and let it penetrate into your heart, my dear little one;
Let nothing discourage you, nothing depress you . . .
Am I not here who am your Mother?

—Our Lady of Guadalupe

There are two pieces of advice on prayer that have meant a great deal to me, and so I pass them on to you. The first is from St. Thérèse. With characteristic audacity she tells us, "We never have too much confidence in the good Lord who is so powerful and merciful. We obtain from Him as much as we hope for" (*Complete Spiritual Doctrine*, 8). I do not think she means that God is limited by our hopes, but rather that His gifts will, at the very least, never fall short of them.

The second bit of advice is just a fragment of wisdom, but it has served me well. It is simply the suggestion to pray as you can, not as you ought. St. Thérèse herself often fell asleep during her prescribed times of prayer. While praying in the chapel she would fall asleep kneeling, and later wake to find her head on the floor once again. This understandably bothered her; after all, her primary vocation as a Carmelite was to pray. But then one day she was inspired to see this awkward situation through the eyes of Love. It occurred to her that parents delight in gazing upon their sleeping children, and so God, the ultimate Father, must delight in seeing His children asleep too. She reminds us as she reminded her sister Leonie, "God is even kinder than you think. He is satisfied with a look, a sigh of love" (*The Little Way of St. Thérèse*, 40).

He truly is entirely good, but He is also awfully big, so in His gentleness He gives us intercessors nearer to our own stature. The following particular prayers to our heavenly friends instill in me a feeling of confidence, and thus they have a Theresian flavor. I have heard that one result of the Fall is we grow tired of receiving. I conclude, then, that we may not be fully prepared for God's abundant gifts in answer to our prayers, but let's live dangerously and ask for our hearts' desires anyhow.

An Old French Prayer for Friends

Blessed Mother of those whose names you can read in my heart, watch over them with every care. Make their way easy and their labors fruitful. Dry their tears if they weep; sanctify their joys; raise their courage if they weaken; restore their hope if they lose heart, their health if they be ill, truth if they err, and repentance if they fall. Amen.

Novena to St. Thérèse

O Little Thérèse of the Child Jesus,
please pick for me a rose from the heavenly gardens
and send it to me as a message of love.

O Little Flower of Jesus, ask God today to grant the favors
I now place with confidence in your hands . . .

St. Thérèse, help me to always believe as you did,
in God's great love for me, so that I might imitate
your Little Way each day. Amen.

Prayer of St. John of the Cross

O blessed Jesus, give me stillness of soul in You.
Let Your mighty calmness reign in me.
Rule me, O You, King of Gentleness, King of Peace.

❧

Prayer to Mary the Undoer of Knots

Virgin Mary, Mother of fair love, Mother who never refuses to come to the aid of a child in need, Mother whose hands never cease to serve your beloved children because they are moved by the divine love and immense mercy that exist in your heart, cast your compassionate eyes upon me and see the snarl of knots that exist in my life. You know very well how desperate I am, my pain and how I am bound by these knots.

Mary, Mother to whom God entrusted the undoing of the knots in the lives of His children, I entrust into your hands the ribbon of my life. No one can take it away from your precious care. In your hands there is no knot that cannot be undone.

Powerful Mother, by your grace and intercessory power with your Son and my Liberator, Jesus, take into your hands today this knot . . . I beg you to undo it for the glory of God, once for all. You are my hope.

O my Lady, you are the sweetest consolation God gives me, the fortification of my feeble strength, the enrichment of my destitution and with Christ the freedom from my chains.

Hear my plea.

Mary, Undoer of Knots, pray for me. Amen.

❧

Prayer to St. Joseph in Every Difficulty

With childlike confidence, I present myself before you, O holy Joseph, faithful foster-father of Jesus! I beg your compassionate intercession and support in this, my present necessity. I firmly believe that you are most powerful near the throne of God, who chose you for the reputed father of His well-beloved Son, Christ Jesus. O blessed Saint, you who saved that Treasure of heaven, along with His virginal Mother, from the rage of His enemies, did with untiring industry supply His earthly wants and with paternal care did accompany and protect Him on all the journeys of His childhood, take me, also, for the love of Jesus, as your child. Assist me in my present difficulty with your prayers before God. The infinite goodness of our Savior who honored and loved you as His father upon earth, cannot refuse you any request now in heaven.

Ah, how many pious souls have sought help from you in their needs, and have experienced to their joy, how good, how mild, how ready to assist you are! How quickly you turn to those who call upon you with confidence! How powerful you are in bringing help and restoring joy to anxious and dejected hearts! Therefore do I fly to you, O most chaste spouse of Mary. Good St. Joseph, I pray you, by the burning love you had for Jesus and Mary upon earth, console me in my distress, and present my petition, through Jesus and Mary, before the throne of God. One word from you will move my good Savior to bless me and to console my afflicted soul. Then, most joyfully shall I praise Him and you, most earnest will be my thanksgivings. Amen.

References

Ahern, Patrick. *Maurice and Thérèse, The Story of a Love*. New York: Doubleday, 1998. Print.

Aquinas, Thomas. *Thomas Aquinas, Selected Writings*. Trans. Ralph McInerny. London: Penguin Books, 1998. Print.

Aristotle. *Basic Works of Aristotle*. Ed. Richard McKeon. New York: Random House, 1941. Print.

Augustine. *Confessions*. Trans. R. S. Pine-Coffin. London: Penguin Books, 1961. Print.

Benedict XVI. "Homily for Mass—World Youth Day XXIII." Catholic Education Resource Center. Web. 1 Feb. 2011.

_____ "Letter to Romans on Education, February 6, 2008." *News Archives*. Catholic Diocese for Chaldeans and Assyrians. Web. 1 Feb. 2011. Http://www.kaldu.org/2008/02/Feb08_08E4.html.

Bosco, John. "Letter From Don Bosco." Salesians International. Web. 31 Jan. 2011. www. Salesians.org.uk/html/letter_from_don_bosco.html.

Catechism of the Catholic Church. New York: Doubleday, 1995. Print.

Champneys, Basil. *Coventry Patmore's Poems*. London: George Bell and Sons, 1906. Print.

Chesterton, G.K. "The Emancipation of Domesticity." *What's Wrong with the World*. Digibooks, 2009. Web. 31 Jan. 2011.

d'Elbeé, Jean C. J. *I Believe in Love*. Manchester, New Hampshire: Sophia Institute Press, 2001. Print.

Dillard, Annie. *The Writing Life*. New York: Harper and Row, 1989. Print.

Holt, John. *What Do I Do Monday*. New York: Boynton Cook, 1995. Print.

______ *How Children Fail*. New York: Da Capo Press, 1995. Print.

______ *How Children Learn*. New York: Da Capo Press, 1995. Print.

Holt, John and P. Farenga. *Teach Your Own, The John Holt Book of Homechooling*. New York: Da Capo Press, 2003. Print.

Jamart, Francois. *Complete Spiritual Doctrine of St. Thérèse of Lisieux*. New York: Alba House, 1961. Print.

John Paul II. *Crossing the Threshold of Hope*. New York: Alfred A. Knopf, 1994. Print.

_______ *Familiaris Consortio*. Washington D.C.: USCCB Publishing,1982. Web. 2 Feb. 2011. www.ewtn.org.

Lewis, C. S. *The Four Loves*. New York: Harcourt Brace Jovanovich, 1960. Print.

Martin, Celine (Sister Geneveive of the Holy Face). *Memoir of My Sister St. Thérèse*. New York: P. J. Kenedy and Sons, 1959. Print.

Martin, Thérèse. *Her Last Conversations*. Trans. John Clarke. Washington D. C.: ICS Publications, 1977. Print.

________ *Story of a Soul*. Trans. John Clarke. Washington D.C.: ICS Publications, 1996. Print.

Mason, Charlotte. *Toward a Philosophy of Education*. Ambleside Online. 1923. Web. 25 Jan. 2011.

_____ *School Education*. Ambleside Online. 1904. Web. 25 Jan. 2011.

_____*Parents and Children*. Ambleside Online. 1896. Web. 25 Jan. 2011.

Mirus, Jeff. "The Blueprint for Heroic Family Life." *In Depth Analysis*. Catholicculture.org. Web 1 Feb. 2011.

Morrison, John A. *The Educational Philosophy of St. John Bosco*. New Rochelle, NY: Don Bosco Publications, 1979. Print.

Nelson, John. *The Little Way of St. Thérèse of Lisieux*. Liguori, Missouri: Ligouri, 1998. Print.

Newman, Cardinal John Henry. *Idea of a University*. Pittsburgh, PA: The National Institute for Newman Studies, 2007. Web. 1 Feb. 2011.

Plato. *The Republic of Plato*. Trans. Allan Bloom. New York: Basic Books Inc., 1968. Print.

Saint John of the Cross. *The Collected Works of St. John of the Cross*. Trans. Kieran Kavanaugh and O. Rodriguez. Washington D.C.: ICS Publications, 1979. Print.

Saxton, Eugene. "St. Giovanni Melchior Bosco." The Catholic Encyclopedia. Vol. 2. New York: Robert Appleton Company, 1907. Web. 17 Feb. 2011. http://www.newadvent.org/cathen/02689d.htm.

The Spirit of St. Thérèse de l'Enfant Jesus. London: Burns, Oates and Washbourne Ltd., 1925. Print.

Weigel, George. "A Better Concept of Freedom." *First Things* 121 (March 2002): 14-20. Catholic Education Resource Center. Web. 1 Feb. 2011.

Wittmann, Maureen. *For the Love of Literature*. La Grange, Kentucky: Ecce Homo Press, 2007. Print.

Acknowledgments

The conversations, the laughter in company, the exchange of affectionate gestures, the shared reading of pleasant literature, common hobbies both frivolous and refined, the occasional disapprovals made without harshness, as everyone does with his own self, and the more frequent approvals. . . .These are what friends find in each other.

—St. Augustine
Confessions

I have saved the best for last. I started with a dedication, and I conclude with a gratitude list.

First I thank my dear ladies: Cindy, Amy, Leonie, Terri, Maria, Beate, Sabine, Susan, Karen, Faith, Lissa, and Willa. Without you this book would not be; with your contributions, it is a many-splendored thing. Thank you for your first immediate "Yes," your writing for me and with me, the gorgeous yellow roses, your prayers, patience, and support.

Next, a heartfelt thank you to the Unschooling Catholics Yahoo group—those who started it and those who keep it going, the regulars and irregulars, posters and lurkers. Your presence inspired this book; your courage, honesty, and faith inspire me. I pray that God continues to bring peace to each of your families.

I offer oceans of appreciation to the four friends who read and listened to me read: Emily, whose sparkling presence is irreplaceable; Mary Anne, whose unconditional love sustains me always; Mary Kate, who boosted the Little Way into the title; and Ann-Marie, whose careful listening saved me from near disaster. Your encouragement and warmth buoyed me up, while your gentle corrections made a big difference. A thousand thanks.

Mike, my husband's paesan, thank you for sharing your time and optimism with us. I don't know which delights me most: your perfect foreword, your unflagging confidence in the book, or your (and Tony's) cousinly excitement over the Serra di Falco connection. I won't choose, I'll just say thank you again for them all.

Stratford and Regina, I am grateful for your kind words and the help you generously gave me; your suggestions improved the book tremendously. I hope our paths continue to cross.

Becher family: Thank you for your example, your neighborliness, your babysitting, your occasional Internet loan, your prayers, and especially for your friendship. God blessed us when He set us down next to you.

Goodrich family: What a thrill for me to finally know a family of Catholic unschoolers face to face. From John Holt to *100 Easy Lessons* to every library in a twenty mile radius, you are a shining example of the genuine article. Thanks for your authenticity, your tea, and your smiles. And Audrey, I am so glad that you loved *Little Women*.

Augros family: Where would the book and I be without your trailer welcome, good cheer (and protein), and help sending the early manuscript to England, no less? May God reward you, and may Amy's laugh ever ring out from our dream house.

Rose, how can I thank you? Your matchmaking, editing, and enthusiasm for this book have been the answer to my prayers. As Susan pointed out to me, you are aptly named.

Dan—I am indebted to you for standing behind Margot in her publishing endeavors. And Margot, I am simply overflowing with gratitude that God sent to me (via Rose) the publisher of my dreams. May you fill the world's shelves with great books, and may Hillside Education prosper.

Ted, thank you from the bottom of my heart for your exquisite cover. Terry and Claire, many thanks for your French and your help in securing the permission for St. Thérèse's photo. And Nora, the interior layout is lovely, surpassed only by the thoughtful way you included me in the process. I am asking St. Thérèse to shower roses upon you all.

All my love and thanks to Joseph, The Catholic Unschooler, and to Dominic, already reminding me, "Mom, trust God!" You guys are the best.

Tony, can you believe that words fail me? "You had to be there," so they say, and you were. "You will have had to have been there," as Gip said, and I look forward to that too.

Oh! And I almost forgot—thank you, St. Thérèse. I believe you that it is all God, but your many words have brought me to Him as He really is: infinitely tender, compassionate Love. Thank you for everything.

See, then, all that Jesus lays claim to from us;
He has no need of our works,
but only of our love . . .

—St. Thérèse, *Story of a Soul*

About the Author/Editor

Suzie Andres is a graduate of Thomas Aquinas College. She has a Master's degree in philosophy from the University of Notre Dame, where she was privileged to study under the gracious Thomists, Joseph Bobik and Ralph McInerny. She and her husband Tony are the proud and bemused parents of two only children; the family has been homeschooling since 1996. This is Suzie's second book. Her first, *Homeschooling with Gentleness, A Catholic Discovers Unschooling* was published by Christendom Press in 2004.

About the Publisher

Margot Davidson, proprietress of Hillside Education, began her publishing career by writing study guides for literature at the request of a friend who was writing a history curriculum for homeschoolers. Writing the guides opened a door for her—a door to possibilities. When the Internet made it easy to track down copyright information, Margot became interested in reprinting historical fiction. She started by reprinting two books she loved and then became addicted to the pleasure that accompanies the creative process of publishing and editing. She counts as a great blessing the opportunity to work with the many talented people who help her to produce works of beauty and goodness for Catholic home educators. Margot and her husband Dan are the parents of five children.

Hillside Education publishes English and composition books, historical fiction reprints, and resources to support Catholic home educators. Please visit www.hillsideeducation.com for a complete listing.

Finis

Printed in the USA
CPSIA information can be obtained
at www.ICGtesting.com
LVHW041929270823
756424LV00002B/273

9 780983 180005